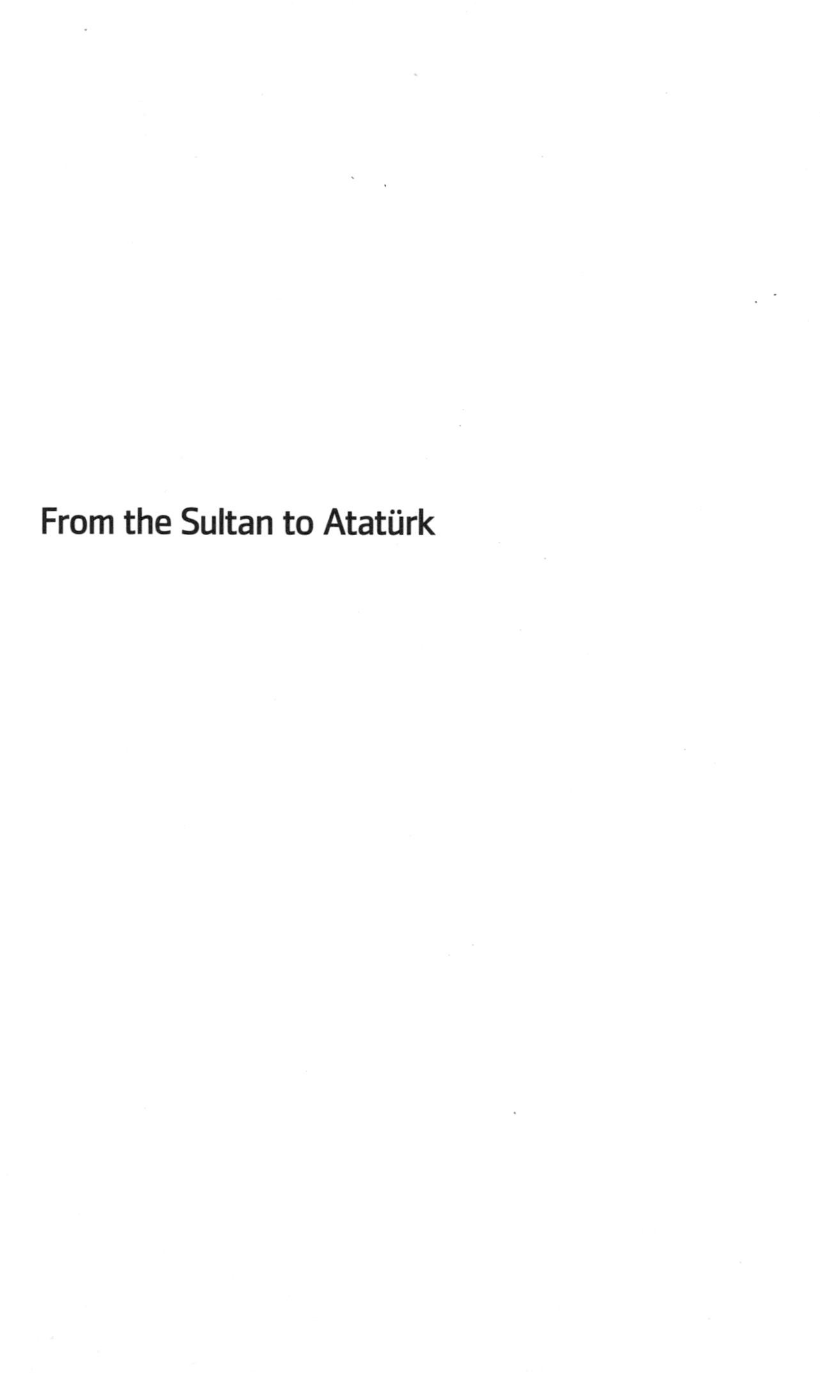

From the Sultan to Atatürk

To Virginia.
Better late than never.
Love
Andrew.
Sept. 2009.

Makers of the Modern World

From the Sultan to Atatürk
Turkey

Andrew Mango

HH
HAUS HISTORIES

First published in Great Britain in 2009 by
Haus Publishing Ltd
70 Cadogan Place
London SW1X 9AH
www.hauspublishing.com

A CIP catalogue record for this book
is available from the British Library

ISBN 978-1-905791-65-1

Series design by Susan Buchanan
Typeset in Sabon by MacGuru Ltd
Printed in Dubai by Oriental Press
Map by Martin Lubikowski, ML Design, London

To the memory of
Professor Metin And

A good friend who wore his learning lightly

Contents

Acknowledgements

My thanks are due to Jaqueline Mitchell, commissioning editor of Haus Publishing, who asked me to write this book, discussed the project in detail and then went carefully through the text and made useful suggestions for corrections and clarifications. I am grateful to the staff of the London Library for locating and allowing me to keep for months books and periodicals I needed to consult and quote. I thank Ahmet Yüksel, the celebrated antiquarian bookseller, whose new premises in Ankara serve as a meeting place for historians in the Turkish capital. Once again I benefited from his rare ability to find out-of-print books. My friends in Turkey, with whom I discussed this book, have helped me with their suggestions and broadened my perspective. Finally, I apologise once again to Mary, who has put up with yet another postponement of my long-overdue retirement and the loss of a summer holiday.

Note on Spelling and Pronunciation

The names and spelling of people and places mentioned in this volume have undergone many changes over time. I have, on the whole, chosen the form currently used and, as such, recognisable to English-speakers today (who fly to Istanbul and not Constantinople, and spend their holidays in Kuşadası and not in the Italianate Scala Nova, and in Antalya and not Adalia). However, historical perspective requires reference to older names and spellings. For places, I have usually given the current name first, followed by the name used by contemporaries of the events described, and, in some cases, the official name in more than one language, e.g. Istanbul/Constantinople, İzmir/Smyrna, İskenderun/Alexandretta, and Meriç/Maritza/Evros for the river which forms the boundary between Greece and Turkey, which is called Meriç in Turkish, Evros in Greek and Maritza in Bulgarian and in Western documents at the time of the settlement after the First World War. However, where a place name occurs frequently, rather than repeat the current Turkish name and the old European form every time, I have sometimes opted for the one or the other, depending on context. Mustafa Kemal did not change the names of the principal cities when he established the Turkish Republic. Istanbul, İzmir, Ankara, Antalya etc. had long been the names by which these places were known to the Turks. What changed after 1923 was the insistence of the Turkish authorities that these forms should also be used by foreigners in their official dealings with Turkey. As a result, European ambassadors who were earlier accredited to the Sultan's government in Constantinople were succeeded by consuls in Istanbul after 1923.

Where names of Turks occur, I give the modern spelling of the given names by which they were known at the time, followed in brackets by the person's surname which came into use when surnames became compulsory in 1934, e.g. Rauf (Orbay), Fethi (Okyar), İsmet (İnönü) etc. For the main hero of the book I have used Mustafa Kemal before 1934, and Atatürk thereafter.

Modern Turkish uses the Latin alphabet and is spelled phonetically. Consonants have roughly the same values as in English, except that:

C is pronounced as j in *joy*
Ç stands for ch in *chair*
Ğ is silent, but lengthens the preceding vowel
H is never silent, and is pronounced as in *he*
J is pronounced as in French *jour*
Ş stands for sh as in *shell*
Y is always a consonant as in *yellow*

Vowels have 'continental' values (similar to those in German). Ö and Ü are pronounced as in German (or as *eu* and *u*) in French. The undotted I (I, ı) represents a sound which does not occur in Western European languages, but does in most Slav languages where it is usually represented by a *y*. The nearest English equivalent would be the phantom vowel in the second syllable of 'rhythm' (spelled in Turkish as *ritım*). I have followed modern Turkish spelling in dotting the capital *İ* as in İsmet, İzmir, etc., except for Istanbul, where a dotted capital *İ* looks pedantic. Most vowels are of uniform length. Where a vowel is long (usually in a word of Arabic or Persian origin) a circumflex (^) is sometimes used to indicate it. Where the vowel 'a' follows the consonants 'k' or 'l', the circumflex shows that the consonant is palatalised (softened), as in Talât (pronounced Tal*ia*t).

One difficulty remains: there is no uniformity in the modern Turkish spelling of names of Arabic origin. I have used etymological spelling for the final consonant e.g. Reşad (not Reşat), but phonetic spelling in the middle of the name, e.g. Vahdettın (and not Vahdeddin or Vahiduddin, Wahid al-Din or any number of other variants, all of which look peculiar in Turkish today).

Mehmed VI Vahdettin (1861–1926).

I

Sèvres

1
Illusions of Power

The First World War destroyed the comfortable certainties of the ruling class throughout Europe. Like the aristocrats who had survived the French Revolution, the rulers of Europe were left with only nostalgic memories of the *douceur de vivre* of the old order. The mass slaughter on the Eastern and the Western Fronts gave the lie to widely-held illusions. Belief in the inexorable progress of civilisation died on European battlefields where the most advanced nations of the world fought each other with the most inhuman weapons and methods they could devise. Barbarians could have done no worse. But other illusions survived. One such was that not all empires were doomed, that while outmoded dynastic empires, like those of the Habsburgs, Romanovs and Ottomans, fell apart, the progressive empires of Britain and France, which had a democratic core, had emerged strengthened by the defeat of their rivals.

When the war ended, Britain, France, Italy and the United States – known as the Principal Allies – thought they could dispose as they wished of the fates and possessions of their enemies. This illusion of omnipotence was disproved first in Russia, then in Turkey and finally and catastrophically in Germany. The emergence of the Bolshevik empire with its centre in Russia, of the Turkish national state and then of the truly evil empire of the Nazis in Germany marked the failure of Allied policies. They had hoped that the First World War would be the war to end all wars, and that it would make the world safe for democracy. These hopes were quickly disappointed. The post-war settlement was short-lived, except in one case. The emergence of a fully independent, stable Turkish national state within the community of civilised nations was a fortunate, if unintended, consequence of the policies of the victors of the War, which we can now see for what it was – a brutal civil war within the Western World.

The Ottoman state entered the fray in 1914 in a reckless gamble by a group of adventurers, led by a triumvirate consisting of two young career officers, Enver and Cemal, and one civilian, Talât. Enver, the leading spirit, was 33 years old in 1914, Cemal was 42 and Talât 40. Enver became Commander-in-Chief (formally Deputy Commander-in-Chief, since the Sultan was nominal C-in-C), Cemal Navy Minister, Commander of the Southern Front and Governor of Syria (which included Lebanon and Palestine), and Talât Minister of the Interior and then Grand Vizier (Prime Minister). These leaders of the Young Turks, as they were known in the West, had risen to power and fame in Ottoman Macedonia in the first decade of the 20th century. Their character had been moulded by their experience in fighting the irregular bands of Balkan nationalists – Slav Macedonians, Bulgarians, Greeks, Serbs and, finally, Albanians. Nationalist irregulars were known in Turkish as *komitacı* (committeemen), a designation which became a byword for ruthlessness, violence and treachery, but also reckless courage. Such men were needed to carve nationally homogeneous states out of a multinational empire – a process which involved massacres, deportations and the flight of millions of refugees. Enver, Cemal and Talât were Turkish *komitacıs* in a literal sense too, as leaders of the Committee of Union and Progress (CUP), whose members were known as Unionists (*İttihatçı*). They were initiated in quasi-Masonic ceremonies in which oaths were sworn on guns and holy books. They conspired against the absolutist regime of Sultan Abdülhamid II, forced him to reintroduce constitutional rule in 1908, deposed him in 1909 and seized power in a coup in 1913. They believed initially that constitutional rule would reconcile all the ethnic communities of the Ottoman Empire and turn them all into loyal Ottoman citizens under the banner of freedom, fraternity and justice. It was their version of the ideals of the French Revolution, which they admired as the Great Revolution. But they admired Napoleon even more and also the German and Japanese militarists whose example confirmed their belief that might was right.

Constitutional rule did unite the nationalists of the Ottoman state – but it united them against the Turks. Sultan Abdülhamid II had preserved his dominions for 30 years by dividing his internal and external enemies. The advent to power of the Young Turks in 1908 prompted the neighbours of the Ottoman state to attack it both singly and jointly. First, nominal Ottoman suzerainty was repudiated in Bosnia-Herzegovina, Bulgaria and Crete; then, in 1911, Italy invaded Tripolitania and Cyrenaica (known today as Libya), the Ottomans' last directly administered territory in Africa; and finally, in 1912, the small Balkan states – Montenegro, Serbia, Bulgaria and Greece – joined forces to end Ottoman rule in Macedonia. The Young Turks scored their only success in

THE CUP TRIUMVIRS

Enver (1881–1922) became a leading member of the Committee of Union and Progress in Salonica, where he was serving as a staff major with the Ottoman Third Army, and won renown as the best-known of the military mutineers who secured the reintroduction of the constitution in 1908. He played a leading role in the suppression of the counter-revolution in Istanbul the following year and, after raising local resistance to the Italians in Cyrenaica, was the main author of the coup which brought the CUP to power in 1913. He married the Sultan's niece in 1914, and became War Minister, Chief of the General Staff and (Deputy) Commander-in-Chief after pushing the Ottoman Empire into the First World War on the side of Germany later that year. Enver was seen as the leading pro-German triumvir, so much so that the Germans referred jokingly to Turkey as 'Enverland'. He fled to Germany in 1918, and after a vain attempt to take over the Turkish resistance movement in Anatolia, moved to Central Asia where he was killed by the Red Army.

Cemal (1872–1922) was the triumvir to whom Mustafa Kemal (Atatürk) was closest. A member of the CUP central committee in Salonica, he restored order in Adana after a bloody anti-Armenian pogrom in 1909, served as Governor of Baghdad, and became Military Governor of Istanbul after the CUP seizure of power in 1913. He was Navy Minister and at the same time Military Governor of Syria and overall Commander of the Southern Front during the First World War. He fled the country in 1918 and was murdered by an Armenian terrorist in Tbilisi (Georgia) in 1922.

Talât (1874–1921) was a lowly post office clerk when he joined the CUP, rising to a leading position within the movement in Salonica. He became Interior Minister in 1913, and was the main author of the deportation of Armenians from Anatolia in 1915. He rose to the top post of Grand Vizier (Prime Minister) in 1917. Along with the other two triumvirs, he escaped in a German warship in 1918, and was assassinated by an Armenian militant in Berlin in 1922.

1913 when the Balkan allies fell out among themselves, allowing Enver to reclaim Edirne (Adrianople) and with it eastern Thrace up to the River Meriç (Maritza/Evros) as the last Ottoman foothold in Europe.

In the West, the Ottoman Empire had long been known as Turkey. In 1914 the Sublime State (its official name in Turkish) had in fact become Turkey-and-Arabia, and even in its remaining territories its hold was uncertain. That year, it had been forced to promise special rule for the six so-called Armenian provinces in eastern Anatolia, where in fact the Armenians were outnumbered by Turks, Kurds and other Muslims. In the Arab provinces there were stirrings, feeble but ominous, of indigenous nationalism, while Turkish troops had to be stationed in the remote (and useless) province of Yemen to keep its feudal ruler under control. The Turkish domestic opponents of the CUP had every right to describe its leaders as bunglers who had promised to safeguard the Ottoman state, but in fact hastened its disintegration. Like unlucky gambling addicts, Enver and his companions pinned their hopes on a new throw of the dice.

Apologists for the Unionist triumvirate have advanced various justifications for their decision to join the Central Powers – Germany and Austria-Hungary. Cemal, they said, had been cold-shouldered when he sought an alliance with France. Britain, they argued, incurred the hostility of the Turks by seizing without compensation two battleships which were being built in British yards with the voluntary subscriptions of Ottoman subjects. But that was in August 1914 when the First Lord of the Admiralty, Winston Churchill, had solid grounds for believing that the CUP leadership had decided to side with Germany. The fact is that the leaders of the CUP wanted to win back some of their losses in the Balkan Wars, and in particular the Greek islands lying off the Turkish coast in the Aegean, that they sought compensation at the expense of Russia in the east for losses they could not retrieve in the west, and that they believed that the Ottoman state had to ally itself with one or the other of the two blocs in order to survive. The CUP leaders had wide-ranging military ambitions, but they lacked the resources to finance them. Germany promised the necessary cash, weapons and technical expertise.

Throughout most of the 19th century the Ottoman state could rely on Britain to keep the Russians out of the Turkish Straits and the imperial capital, Constantinople/Istanbul. But in 1908 in order to counter the threat of German domination of Europe, Britain recruited Russia in support of its *entente cordiale* with France.[1] On the eve of the war in 1914, a plan backed by Russia to appoint a Christian or European governor for an 'Armenian province' was blocked by Germany, thanks to whose mediation the governor became, less objectionably, an inspector-general. By entering the war on the side of Germany, the Young Turks got rid of the inspector-general.[2] But Turkey could have achieved the same result, if not more, by playing off Germany against the Triple Entente without committing itself to either side. Instead, it concluded an alliance with Germany under the cloak of neutrality and then launched an attack on the Russian fleet in the Black Sea without a preliminary declaration of war, setting a precedent for Pearl Harbor. The Ottoman cabinet was not even informed of this act of aggression which was staged by the Unionist triumvirate.

The Ottoman state thus became the eastern wing of the German-Austro-Hungarian alliance. Its communications with Germany were made safe when Bulgaria joined the Central Powers in order to make good its losses in the Second Balkan War, and when Serbia (whose nationalists had ignited the fuse of the conflict) was overrun at the end of 1915. But while the railway line from Berlin to Istanbul was adequate, communications between the Ottoman capital and its eastern and southern fronts relied on the unfinished single-track Baghdad railway built by the Germans. As the tunnels through the Taurus mountains were not completed until the end of the war, men and supplies had to cross the range on foot and on pack animals. The line ended at the northern edge of the desert between Syria and Mesopotamia, a long way from the Russian front. In the south too there were big gaps in the railway network between Aleppo and the Egyptian frontier, where the Ottomans faced British imperial forces.

There was little industry in the Ottoman state, which could just about manufacture uniforms for its troops, and simple small arms. In the 19th century, the Ottomans had entered the world economy as exporters of handicrafts, such as carpets, and of cash crops, mainly tobacco and dried fruit. Even in peacetime, Istanbul relied on imported Russian grain, sugar and tea. In wartime, as the country's largely rural economy was disrupted by conscription and military operations, malnutrition was widespread and starvation a constant danger.

According to official statistics, the total population of the state was 18.5 million, of whom 15 million were Muslims – Turks, Arabs, Kurds and others. British sources put the total higher – at 21.5 million for the Asian provinces alone. In the census, people were classified by religion and not by ethnic origin or mother tongue. However, an analysis of provincial statistics suggests that the number of Arabic-speakers was probably around six million, and of Kurds two to three million. Nomadic tribal Kurds and Arab Bedouin eked out a meagre subsistence by breeding sheep, goats and camels, and by extorting protection money from the state, from travellers and from settled populations generally. But even in the relatively advanced provinces, some 90 per cent of the Muslims were illiterate. Tuberculosis, malaria, and trachoma (an eye

The Ottoman Empire 1914

RUSSIA
Poti
Batumi
Tbilisi
Kars
Erivan
Trabzon
Erzurum
Caspian Sea
Araks
Van
Lake Van
Lake Urmia
EMPIRE
PERSIA
Tigris
Euphrates
Samara
Baghdad
Ctesiphon
Kut el Amara
Basra
0
300 kilometres

disease which causes blindness) were endemic. Average life expectancy was 30 years. In wartime malnutrition, typhus and typhoid took a heavy toll.

However, the backwardness of the Asian provinces, which made up the bulk of the state, could be easily forgotten in the cosmopolitan centres – the capital, Constantinople/Istanbul, and the port cities of Smyrna/İzmir on the Aegean and of Trebizond/Trabzon on the Black Sea. In the capital, non-Muslims made up 40 per cent of a population of approximately one million, and dominated trade and the professions. In Smyrna, nicknamed 'infidel İzmir' by the Turks, there were more Christians than Muslims.[3] Istanbul and İzmir were European cities, with good schools, theatres, electric trams and gas lighting. Istanbul was a world in itself, where magnificent monuments from the city's past – mosques, palaces, but also rich mansions – fostered illusions of grandeur. These illusions were not confined to Turks and other Muslims.

The Greeks who made up the second largest community in Istanbul, and were present in large numbers along the coasts of the Aegean and the Black Sea, had seen their numbers, prosperity and economic power rise throughout the 19th century. The more ambitious among them dreamt of replacing the Turks as rulers of a revived Byzantine Empire. Armenian nationalists disregarded the numerical weakness of their community, which numbered one and a half to two million,[4] and set their hopes on restoring the mediaeval Armenian kingdom in eastern and southern Turkey. Of course not all the Greeks and Armenians were nationalists, but the Ottoman state could not rely on the loyalty even of those in the Christian communities who had prospered under its rule.

Nevertheless the Ottoman state punched well above its weight. This was partly due to the hardihood and courage of Turkish conscripts. 'The Turkish peasant will hide under his mother's skirts to avoid conscription, but once in uniform he will fight like a lion,' a Russian expert on Turkey wrote during the war.[5] But there was another reason to which most Western observers were blind and which historians have come to notice only recently. While the rural masses were illiterate and ignorant of the modern world, there was an elite of experienced and well-trained Turkish civil servants and army officers. Although the reforms of the 19th century (known as the *Tanzimat*, meaning 'the (re)ordering') were routinely decried in the West as inadequate and a sham, by the beginning of the 20th century Ottoman administration compared well with that of other contemporary empires – so much so that many of its former subjects came to regret its eventual dissolution. A recent study suggests that in the Arab lands placed under British and French Mandates at the end of the First World War, there was little improvement for indigenous Muslims in such basic areas as average life expectancy, education, communications and public order.[6] Ottoman civil administration was organised on French lines, while in the army French and British advisers were largely replaced by Germans from the reign of Abdülhamid II onwards. The efficiency of Ottoman governors and commanders was often overlooked by Western critics who decried their rule as backward and corrupt. Foreign observers also overlooked the fact that many of the Greeks, particularly along the Aegean coast, were immigrants from the newly-independent Greek kingdom who found life under Ottoman rule more rewarding than in their own country.

Enver and his associates were poor diplomats and bad judges of the national interest. But after the disaster of the Balkan Wars they reorganised the army and turned it into an efficient fighting force, if only to waste it in ill-planned operations. A symbolic explosion marked the declaration of war: a monument erected by the Russians in the Istanbul suburb of San Stefano (today's Yeşilköy, the site of the modern Atatürk airport) where the Tsarist empire had imposed a peace treaty on the defeated Ottomans in 1878, was blown up and its destruction filmed for Turkey's first newsreel. As Caliph of the Muslims worldwide, the Sultan – the elderly Mehmed V who did as he was told by the CUP – proclaimed the *jihad* – a holy war against the Allies. There were doubts that fighting as junior partner of two Christian empires against three other Christian empires could count as a *jihad*. In any case, Muslims took little notice of the proclamation – Indian Muslims continued to fight in the ranks of the British army, Algerian and Senegalese Muslims in the French army, while the Tsar's 'wild cavalry' depended as ever on Muslim horsemen. As for Arab Bedouins, they kept to their tradition of serving the most generous paymaster – and the British easily outbid the Ottomans.

Mehmed V Reşad (1844–1918) acceded to the Ottoman throne in 1909, when his elder brother Abdülhamid II was deposed by the Young Turks. A pious and mild man, who sympathised with the Sufi Whirling Dervishes, he was the country's first constitutional Sultan. Throughout most of his reign this meant that he did the Young Turks' bidding. His only reported criticism of the Young Turk war leader Enver Pasha was a remark after a meal. 'The Pasha drinks water when he eats leeks. It is unheard of.'

In the winter of 1914/15, Enver led an Ottoman army to destruction in the snows of the mountains of eastern Anatolia on the Caucasian front, which stretched far from the nearest Ottoman railhead, but lay conveniently close to the Russian broad-gauge rail network. In the south, Cemal pushed to the Suez Canal, which some of his units managed to cross, but the Egyptians failed to rise against their British overlords who drove the Turks back into Palestine. Unsuccessful in their attacks, the Turkish army then scored two notable victories in defensive battles. It beat back the British-Anzac and French attempt to break through the Gallipoli peninsula to Istanbul in 1915, and checked a British advance from Basra to Baghdad the following year, surrounding a British force and forcing it to surrender at Kut al-Amara. It was the high point of the Ottoman war effort, which had an effect on Allied perceptions. The British army came to respect 'Johnny Turk' as a good fighter, but Allied governments and diplomats vowed revenge: the Turks' successful defence of Gallipoli and their dogged resistance in Mesopotamia (today's Iraq) and Palestine had prolonged the war and vastly increased its cost in casualties and resources. Allied statesmen, whose miscalculations had been exposed, became determined to eliminate once and for all the danger which, they believed, the Turks posed to their empires. This difference in perceptions between soldiers and civilians was to play an important part in post-war developments, which showed that the soldiers had the more realistic view of Turkey's strength.

The bloody battles in Gallipoli, in which each side lost a quarter of a million men killed and wounded, laid the foundations of the career of a young Turkish officer with political ambitions. Staff Colonel Mustafa Kemal was 34 years old at the time and had with some difficulty secured the command of a Turkish division held in reserve on the peninsula when the British and Anzacs landed on 25 April 1915. Born in Salonica in 1881, he had taken an active part in military plots aimed at forcing Sultan Abdülhamid II to reintroduce the Ottoman constitution of 1876. When the First World War broke out, he was known as an independent-minded Unionist and a critic of Enver and of the subservience of the Ottoman army to the Germans. Nevertheless his initiative and personal courage which helped contain the first Allied landings, impressed Field Marshal Liman von Sanders,[7] the German commander of the Ottoman troops at Gallipoli, and when the British made a second landing on the peninsula at Souvla Bay, Kemal was appointed commander of the forces which held the line against them. Later legend has it that Kemal's rising star was noticed immediately by friend and foe alike. In fact the British did not distinguish him from other Ottoman commanders, and Enver denied him publicity in Turkey. But he won appreciation where it mattered – among other Turkish commanders. Mustafa Kemal resisted German interference in Turkish military dispositions and left Gallipoli in a huff before the Allied withdrawal in December 1915. Promoted Brigadier – the highest rank he was to achieve during the War – he was given the command of an army corps which was being laboriously transferred to the Eastern Front in order to halt the Russian advance. He arrived in an area devastated by the fighting and by the deportation of the Armenians who had dominated it economically.

Armenian nationalist revolutionaries had originally joined the Young Turks in the ranks of the opposition to Abdülhamid II. But after the reintroduction of the constitution in 1908 their ways parted. While the Young Turks' ideal was equality in a centralised state, the demands of Armenian, as of other Christian nationalists, ranged from the recognition of special rights through autonomy to outright independence for their community. Unlike Ottoman Greeks and Bulgarians, Ottoman Armenians had no existing national state which they could join. But when the Russians conquered the Caucasus, and particularly after the Russian gains at the expense of the Ottomans in 1878, the number of Armenian subjects of the Tsar increased, as Armenians long resident in the Caucasus were joined by immigrants from Turkey, who found greater scope for their energies under Christian Russian rule.

According to Armenian sources, in 1912 there were some 1.3 million Armenians in 'Russian Armenia' (the Caucasian provinces) against one million in 'Turkish Armenia'.[8] True, there were tensions between the Armenians and their Tsarist rulers who favoured their own version of Eastern Orthodox Christianity over the Armenian (Monophysite) Gregorian Church, and who fitfully pursued a policy of Russifying their subjects. Even so, as Christians, the Armenians had more in common with the Russians than with Muslim Turks, and although by the end of the 19th century they did well in both the Ottoman and the Tsarist empires, the latter was more advanced and opportunities in it accordingly more promising. The decision of the Young Turks to throw in their lot with the Germans against the Russians was a tragedy for the Armenians who found themselves divided between the two combatants. The majority kept their heads down. But for nationalist Armenian revolutionaries who had used terrorism first against their own kinsmen to gain control over them, then against the Ottoman state and occasionally against Tsarist officials they disliked, the Ottomans' calamity was the Armenians' opportunity. Disaster threatened to overwhelm the Ottoman state in 1915 when the Western Allies landed in Gallipoli and the Russians advanced deep into eastern Turkey. Armenian revolutionaries had been preparing for that day. They had infiltrated fighters and stockpiled arms in eastern Turkey; they had formed volunteer units to help the Russian army. As the Russians advanced, Armenian nationalist revolutionaries organised uprisings and acts of sabotage behind the Ottoman lines.[9] This compromised the Armenian community as a whole. In April 1915, the Young Turk leadership – and Talât in particular – became convinced that the removal of all Armenians from the war zone and from the vicinity of the railways leading to it was a military necessity. It would also remove once and for all the threat of losing yet another portion of the Turkish homeland to local Christians who, as experience showed, would, if successful, get rid of their Muslim neighbours by fair means or foul. For centuries Muslims and Christian Armenians had lived in reasonable amity side by side to their mutual benefit. Now fear and hatred gripped both communities, many of whose members became convinced that they were faced with a stark choice: kill or be killed.

Large-scale deportations have not been rare in history. The Ottomans had transferred their unruly kinsmen, the Turcoman tribesmen, from Asia to their new conquests in the Balkans; they had also moved Christian Armenians and others to repopulate Istanbul after the conquest. They had received Jews and Arabs deported from Spain after the *reconquista*, and then from the 18th century onwards, hundreds of thousands of Muslims forced out of the Balkans, southern Russia and the Caucasus.[10]

In the 19th century, more than a million Circassians were expelled by the Russians from the Caucasus. Hundreds of thousands of them perished before they could start a new life in the Ottoman Empire. Many of the survivors were resettled in eastern Anatolia, which Armenian nationalists were claiming for themselves. The Circassians were a martial people: some of the refugees preyed on settled Ottoman subjects, others found employment in the Ottoman army and gendarmerie. In 1915, as the Russians threatened them again in their new homes, discipline could not restrain the Circassian gendarmes. In some instances, instead of protecting Armenians during the deportation, they killed them. In any case, the best-trained gendarmes had been sent to the front and their duties in the Ottoman countryside had been taken over by raw recruits, including released convicts. There were instances where gendarmes escorting columns of deported Armenians sold them to Kurdish tribesmen who robbed, and then killed the Armenians and raped their women. Undisciplined gendarmes, Kurdish tribesmen and bandits of all sorts, whose numbers had been swollen by deserters, took a heavy toll of the deportees. Others died of malnutrition and disease, which affected even larger numbers of Muslims, for as Armenian civilians were driven south to Syria, at least as many Muslim civilians – Kurds and Turks alike – were fleeing west from the advancing Russians and their Armenian auxiliaries.

In absolute numbers more Muslims than Armenians perished in Anatolia, but while Armenian deaths from all causes accounted for more than a third of their community, the Muslims lost one-fifth, and remained in possession of the land. Moreover, the sufferings of the Armenians were well documented. There were American missionaries and consuls in the area, as the United States was not at war with the Ottoman Empire; German officers and civilians also witnessed atrocities. But the sufferings of the Muslim population passed largely unnoticed by Western observers.

Brigadier Mustafa Kemal was successful in the initial phase of the operation planned by Enver to attack the invading Russians from the north and the south. In the 1916 campaigning season Kemal's troops recaptured two towns – Muş and Bitlis – south of Lake Van on the east Anatolian plateau. But Enver's pincer operation failed, and the Russians retook Muş.

As winter set in, the Russian front stabilised, and Mustafa Kemal was given a command on the Syrian front against the British under the German commander Erich von Falkenhayn, who had been Chief of the General Staff when the German army launched its costly, unsuccessful assault on the French at Verdun. Kemal quickly decided that von Falkenhayn was serving German and not Ottoman interests. Once again he resigned his command and returned to Istanbul. He was then sent off out of harm's way in the suite of the Ottoman heir apparent Mehmed Vahdettin who had been invited to visit the Germans' western front in France. By then Russia was out of the war.

Soon after the first Russian Revolution in February 1917, the Tsarist army disintegrated. On the Caucasian front, territory seized by the Russians, who had made some attempts to prevent inter-communal killings, was taken over by Armenian militias. The militias avenged themselves on local Muslims for the fate of their kinsmen deported two years previously. Then, after the Bolshevik Revolution in November 1917, the Soviet government sued for peace and was forced to accept the loss of the western portion of the Tsarist empire (from Finland through Poland to the Ukraine), and, subject to a referendum, territory the Russians had gained from the Ottomans in 1878.

The collapse of Russia, a full year before the collapse of Germany in November 1918, tempted Enver into another adventure. Ottoman troops had earlier been despatched to Galicia (now divided between Poland and Ukraine) to reinforce the Austro-Hungarians against the Russians. Just as the front held by the Ottomans against the British in Palestine and Mesopotamia was about to crumble, Enver withdrew more troops from it and ordered them to move into the Caucasus beyond the 1878 Russian frontier. He overrode the objections of the Germans who had their own plans for a puppet government in Georgia and for control of the oilfields in Baku (held precariously by a British force after the Russian collapse). As he pursued his dream of a Turkic empire stretching all the way to central Asia and eyed territories about which he was woefully ill-informed, Enver weakened the defence of the Turkish core of the empire – Anatolia and eastern Thrace.

The elderly, weak-willed Sultan Mehmed V (Mehmed Reşad) died in July 1918. He was succeeded by his younger brother, the 57-year-old Vahdettin, who took the title of Mehmed VI. Mustafa Kemal had made a favourable impression on him earlier that year during their tour of the Western Front. They were both critical of the Unionist leadership and their conduct of the war. Vahdettin thought he could use Kemal, while Kemal banked on the favour of his new sovereign for his own designs. While Vahdettin was vacillating, suspicious, ill-informed, woolly-minded and fearful for the safety of his throne, Kemal was clear-headed and realistic. This allowed him to turn the relationship to his advantage. It was also Kemal who had the clearer grasp of the Ottomans' military weakness, which he witnessed in August 1918 when he accepted a command on the Syrian front, this time under his old commander Liman von Sanders. A year earlier, when he had refused to serve under von Falkenhayn, Kemal had urged on the Ottoman high command in Istanbul the urgent need to withdraw troops from Galicia, renounce Enver's Caucasian adventure, and concentrate all available forces for the defence of Anatolia. By the time Kemal returned to Syria, a month after Vahdettin's accession to the throne, the position of the Ottoman forces had become desperate. Jerusalem had been lost to General Allenby's British Imperial forces the previous December, and a weakened Ottoman army was trying to hold a line in northern Palestine, with headquarters in Nazareth. The British broke through in September, a month after Kemal's arrival on the front. Thereafter his main concern was to escape capture and to save as many of his troops as he could for the defence of Anatolia.

By the autumn of 1918, out of the total of 2.85 million men conscripted in the Ottoman Empire during the war, only 560,000 still bore arms, and of these only a quarter were available for combat. Some of the best troops – eight well-equipped divisions at full strength – had been despatched to the Caucasus and northern Persia, where they could not affect the course of the war. Half a million deserters roamed the interior of Anatolia.[11] As the military situation worsened, talk of a separate peace began to be heard in Istanbul. President Woodrow Wilson's peace proposals seemed to offer a way out. In a speech to Congress in January 1918 Wilson had formulated the principles which, he believed, should inspire peacemaking. He set them out in the Fourteen Points, of which the Twelfth declared: 'The Turkish portion of the present Ottoman Empire should be assured a secure sovereignty, but the other nationalities which are now under Turkish rule should be assured an undoubted security of life and an absolutely unmolested opportunity of autonomous development, and the Dardanelles should be permanently opened as a free passage to the ships and commerce of all nations under international guarantees.'

This was not a bad bargaining offer to the embattled Ottomans. Moreover, the rhetoric of President Wilson and of the Young Turks coincided in one important respect: Disregarding the fact that they were fighting to save an empire, the Young Turks had posed as the champions of the peoples of the East against the imperialists. Wilson seemed to echo them. Although by then the United States was fighting on the side of the British and French empires, Wilson proclaimed loftily: 'In regard to these essential rectifications of wrong and assertions of right, we feel ourselves to be intimate partners of all the governments and peoples associated together against the imperialists.'[12] No wonder that as they tried to avert the impending catastrophe, many Ottoman patriots saw a lifeline in Wilson's principles. Moreover, Wilson's Twelfth Point echoed the statement made a few days earlier by the British Prime Minister, David Lloyd George. The Allies, he said, were not fighting 'to deprive Turkey of its capital, or of the rich and renowned lands of Asia Minor and Thrace, which are predominantly Turkish by race'.[13]

In a first response in February 1918, the Ottoman foreign minister agreed that the diverse nationalities in the empire should be granted their own institutions.[14] In spite of reverses in the field and weakening morale, the Ottomans still wielded considerable bargaining power at the time. But the Unionist leadership was unable to make up its mind on how to end the disastrous war into which they had led the country. Enver still believed in a German victory and kept Talât Pasha's cabinet in the dark about the worsening situation on the front. Even the defeat of the last German offensive on the Western Front in July 1918 did not shake the government out of its indecision. The opportunity to make peace on favourable terms was lost.

On 15 September, the Bulgarian army crumbled before the assault of the Allied forces in Macedonia. Four days later General Allenby scattered the Turkish troops holding the front in northern Palestine. Talât Pasha had earlier gone to Berlin to discuss a united response of the Central Powers to

PRESIDENT WILSON'S FOURTEEN POINTS, 8 JANUARY 1918

The program of the world's peace, therefore, is our program; and that program, the only possible program, as we see it, is this:

I. Open covenants of peace, openly arrived at, after which there shall be no private international understandings of any kind but diplomacy shall proceed always frankly and in the public view.

II. Absolute freedom of navigation upon the seas, outside territorial waters, alike in peace and in war, except as the seas may be closed in whole or in part by international action for the enforcement of international covenants.

III. The removal, so far as possible, of all economic barriers and the establishment of an equality of trade conditions among all the nations consenting to the peace and associating themselves for its maintenance.

IV. Adequate guarantees given and taken that national armaments will be reduced to the lowest point consistent with domestic safety.

V. A free, open-minded, and absolutely impartial adjustment of all colonial claims, based upon a strict observance of the principle that in determining all such questions of sovereignty the interests of the populations concerned must have equal weight with the equitable claims of the government whose title is to be determined.

VI. The evacuation of all Russian territory and such a settlement of all questions affecting Russia as will secure the best and freest cooperation of the other nations of the world in obtaining for her an unhampered and unembarrassed opportunity for the independent determination of her own political development and national policy and assure her of a sincere welcome into the society of free nations under institutions of her own choosing; and, more than a welcome, assistance also of every kind that she may need and may herself desire. The treatment accorded Russia by her sister nations in the months to come will be the acid test of their good will, of their comprehension of her needs as distinguished from their own interests, and of their intelligent and unselfish sympathy.

VII. Belgium, the whole world will agree, must be evacuated and restored, without any attempt to limit the sovereignty which she enjoys in common with all other free nations. No other single act will serve as this will serve to restore confidence among the nations in the laws which they

have themselves set and determined for the government of their relations with one another. Without this healing act the whole structure and validity of international law is forever impaired.

VIII. All French territory should be freed and the invaded portions restored, and the wrong done to France by Prussia in 1871 in the matter of Alsace-Lorraine, which has unsettled the peace of the world for nearly fifty years, should be righted, in order that peace may once more be made secure in the interest of all.

IX. A readjustment of the frontiers of Italy should be effected along clearly recognizable lines of nationality.

X. The peoples of Austria-Hungary, whose place among the nations we wish to see safeguarded and assured, should be accorded the freest opportunity to autonomous development.

XI. Rumania, Serbia, and Montenegro should be evacuated; occupied territories restored; Serbia accorded free and secure access to the sea; and the relations of the several Balkan states to one another determined by friendly counsel along historically established lines of allegiance and nationality; and international guarantees of the political and economic independence and territorial integrity of the several Balkan states should be entered into.

XII. The Turkish portion of the present Ottoman Empire should be assured a secure sovereignty, but the other nationalities which are now under Turkish rule should be assured an undoubted security of life and an absolutely unmolested opportunity of autonomous development, and the Dardanelles should be permanently opened as a free passage to the ships and commerce of all nations under international guarantees.

XIII. An independent Polish state should be erected which should include the territories inhabited by indisputably Polish populations, which should be assured a free and secure access to the sea, and whose political and economic independence and territorial integrity should be guaranteed by international covenant.

XIV. A general association of nations must be formed under specific covenants for the purpose of affording mutual guarantees of political independence and territorial integrity to great and small states alike.

Wilson's peace terms. Unable to agree among themselves, the Central Powers sued for peace separately. The first to collapse was Bulgaria. Passing through the Bulgarian capital, Sofia, on his way back home, Talât Pasha witnessed the disintegration of the army which had guarded the western approaches to Istanbul. The game was up. Talât acknowledged this with characteristic bluntness, saying 'We have eaten shit!'[15] Four years later, Sir Horace Rumbold, British High Commissioner in the Ottoman capital, was to use the same image, in a slightly more polite form. 'If the Greeks crack,' he wrote, 'we may expect to eat dirt to an unlimited extent and this is not a form of diet that has ever agreed with me, though Pellé [the French High Commissioner] and Garroni [his Italian counterpart] may flourish on it.'[16] But no one, and least of all Lloyd George, expected such a reversal of fortune when the Allies emerged triumphant from the First World War.

'If the Greeks crack we may expect to eat dirt to an unlimited extent and this is not a form of diet which has ever agreed with me.'
HORACE RUMBOLD

Talât's cabinet finally resigned on 13 October. On the same day Enver sent a last message to all Ottoman forces urging them to prevent the loss of any more Turkish territory before the conclusion of an armistice.[17] The CUP was finally out of office. But it still held the majority of seats in parliament, which could once again exercise its powers under the constitution. The CUP also controlled the security forces in the capital and dominated the provinces through its local organisations. In opposition, in power and then again in opposition, the CUP represented modernity. Nationalism was the dominant ideology in the world, and Wilson's advocacy of the self-determination of nations confirmed its legitimacy. In the crumbling Ottoman state, it was the CUP which championed Muslim nationalism as it melded into Turkish nationalism. There were few men of experience in politics, the administration or the army who had not collaborated with the Unionists in the ranks of the opposition to Sultan Abdülhamid. Later, most of them had served Unionist governments or been members of the CUP. In the circumstances, it was the critics of the leadership within the party, and particularly of its decision to side with Germany in the war, who took over from the defeated Unionist triumvirate.

Talât was succeeded by a distinguished soldier, Ahmed İzzet Pasha, an outspoken opponent of the war policy of the triumvirate, who had nevertheless served with distinction as overall commander of the Caucasian front before the Russian Revolution. Ahmed İzzet was a bluff German-trained officer of Albanian origin, born in Macedonia. His long-standing association with the Germans showed in his moustache in the style of Kaiser Wilhelm II. More importantly, he was attached to the Ottoman dynasty with all the strength of the Albanian ideal of *besa* – the tradition of total loyal commitment to a patron. When an Albanian state emerged in 1913 from the Ottoman defeat in the Balkan wars, he was offered the position of head of state as Prince of Albania. Ahmed İzzet refused, saying that it would be a step down for a servant of the Ottoman Sultan. It was, as the Turkish saying had it, 'to dismount a horse in order to ride a donkey'.

Ahmed İzzet's cabinet included three prominent Unionist critics of the triumvirate: Cavid, who as Finance Minister had extracted every penny he could from Enver's German allies, Fethi (who later took the surname Okyar), an early political patron of Mustafa Kemal, and a naval officer, Rauf (later Orbay), who had risen to fame during the Balkan Wars as captain of the Ottoman cruiser *Hamidiye*, evading capture as she raided the coasts of the Balkan allies. While German influence was strong in the army, the Ottoman navy, which had British advisers before the war, was traditionally pro-British, and Rauf felt, as it proved, an exaggerated confidence in British good intentions.

Mustafa Kemal, who was busy reorganising the remnants of Ottoman forces on the Syrian front, had sensed that a change of government was necessary to end the hostilities. Presuming on his friendship with the new Sultan Vahdettin, he advised him to appoint Ahmed İzzet Pasha Grand Vizier, and asked for himself the post of War Minister. The telegram was delayed, and Ahmed İzzet was appointed without the benefit of Mustafa Kemal's advice. As a professional soldier, the new Grand Vizier preferred to keep the post of War Minister for himself.

The first job of the new Ottoman government was to establish contact with the Allies. The abject condition of the country showed through the high-flown Ottoman chancery rhetoric of the decree appointing Ahmed İzzet to the post of Grand Vizier: 'Whereas it is our most particular wish that the effects produced by the present war, which has been waged with extreme violence for more than four years, on the general affairs of our dominions and their good order and discipline should be rectified, and that concord and general amity should be established among all classes of our people, it is our expectation that you apply your well-known zeal and devote the greatest care to the choice of powerful and efficient measures to obtain the means to bring to a successful conclusion the political initiatives we have undertaken in order to achieve these aims and, at the same time, to secure the supremacy of religious and civil law, the stability of safe and orderly government, to make perfect the condition of ease and well-being of our people, supplying them with the necessities of life without further delay and facilitating the satisfaction of general needs.'[18] In other words, the country is prey to anarchy and lawlessness, people are at each other's throats, they are at their wits' ends with hunger and privation. Please do something about it quickly, and make sure that the Allies respond to our political overtures.

At the beginning of October the Sultan had sent a personal representative to Bern who arranged that the agent of an Armenian Ottoman dignitary Boghos Nubar Pasha should communicate his peace terms to the British minister in Switzerland, Sir Horace Rumbold. Vahdettin proposed that the Arab provinces should become autonomous under his suzerainty, that the Greek islands off Turkey's Aegean coast should be returned to the Ottoman state along with Bulgarian gains in the Balkan Wars, that the British should help him destroy the CUP and should maintain him on the throne. In exchange he offered an alliance with Britain and reforms under British control.[19] In other words, if the British made good the territorial losses the Ottoman Empire had suffered under the rule of the Young Turks, he was prepared to place himself under British protection. What Vahdettin did not realise was that while he was ready to trade the independence of his state for its nominal territorial integrity and his survival as Sultan, his subjects had other ideas. So too had the British who were already in possession of the Ottomans' Arab provinces. Nubar Pasha, on whose good offices the Sultan relied, was soon afterwards to demand from the Allies a large slice of Ottoman territory for an independent Armenian state.

A few days later, the British received a similar offer from an independent-minded Unionist, Rahmi, who had run İzmir and the surrounding country as his personal fiefdom during the war, had protected the large community of Allied subjects who lived and traded there and had prevented the deportation of Armenians from the area. Rahmi had one additional request – that Britain should replace Germany as Turkey's paymaster by guaranteeing the Ottoman currency. Where the Sultan had used an Armenian, Rahmi had used a Greek as an intermediary.[20] Neither realised that the days of the multi-ethnic Ottoman state were numbered, and that the employment of local Christians to represent the Ottoman state could no longer conciliate either the Allies or the local Christian communities. These two attempts to initiate peace talks failed.

Ahmed İzzet had better luck. This time the intermediary was the British General, Sir Charles Townshend, who had surrendered to the Turks after a six-month siege at Kut al-Amara in Mesopotamia in the spring of 1916. While 70 per cent of the 3,000 British rank-and-file who surrendered in Kut died in captivity – many during death marches through the desert, others due to appalling conditions in POW camps[21] – Townshend was held in a comfortable villa on the island resort of Prinkipo/Büyükada, the largest of the Princes' Islands in the Sea of Marmara near Istanbul. He had even been invited to tea by Enver. When he heard that Ahmed İzzet was forming a new cabinet, Townshend offered to transmit the Ottoman peace proposals to Admiral Sir Somerset Calthorpe, commander of the British Mediterranean Fleet, who had his headquarters on the Greek island of Lemnos in the Aegean.

On 16 October, the Ottoman cabinet decided to seek a separate peace, after hearing a report on the military situation. 'We have six or seven thousand men left on each front [Syria, Mesopotamia and Thrace],' the Ottoman General Staff told Ahmet İzzet's cabinet. 'It's so bad you could invade the country with a handful of bandits.'[22] The delay in facing military facts had bred an exaggerated pessimism which was to weaken the hand of Ottoman negotiators. The following day, Ahmed İzzet received Townshend and accepted his offer to go to Lemnos. But, first of all, the composition of the Ottoman delegation and its instructions had to be decided. This did not prove easy. The Sultan, fearful and suspicious as ever, complicated matters.

On 23 October Admiral Calthorpe informed the Ottoman government that he had been authorised to sign an armistice on behalf of the Allies. On hearing this, Ahmed İzzet sought the Sultan's approval for a delegation led by the Ottoman army commander in İzmir, the port from which the Ottoman emissaries would set off for Lemnos. The Sultan disagreed and asked that the chief of the delegation should be his brother-in-law, Damad Ferid Pasha. (*Damad* means son-in-law, and the title was conferred on Ferid when he became the second husband of Mediha, the daughter of Sultan Vahdettin's father, Abdülmecid I.) 'The man is mad,' objected Ahmet İzzet.[23] He was not the first to say so.

Ferid's highest job in the Ottoman civil service had been that of First Secretary at the Ottoman embassy in London. When in 1888 Mediha had asked the reigning Sultan Abdülhamid II (Vahdettin's elder brother) to send Ferid back to London, this time as ambassador, he had replied: 'Sister, the London embassy is not a school, it's an important embassy and the appointment should go to somebody who has experience and understanding of international politics.'[24] Later, when the CUP came to power, Ferid extolled it to the skies. But as he failed to win promotion, he joined the opposition Liberty and Concord Party (known in the West as Liberal Union). Here too he was unlucky. When the CUP was briefly out of power at the beginning of the Balkan Wars, the Sultan proposed that Ferid should head the delegation to the peace talks in London. Ferid refused, saying that he could not sign away any part of Ottoman territory, as this would violate the Constitution. 'The man is mad', said the elderly Grand Vizier Kâmil Pasha, who knew that territorial losses were inevitable. Ferid thereafter twiddled his thumbs in his wife's mansion on the Bosphorus. Where in Britain politics often revolved round the country houses of the aristocracy, in the late Ottoman Empire political decisions were taken and plots hatched in *yalıs*, wooden seaside mansions of princes and pashas on the shores of the Bosphorus. In later years many of these *yalıs* were burned down. A few survive in the hands of business tycoons. Damad Ferid's (or rather his wife's) *yalı* now houses a restaurant patronised by university professors.

At the Sultan's insistence, Ahmed İzzet called on Damad Ferid and heard out his views on the armistice. 'As soon as I see the Admiral [Calthorpe],' Damad Ferid declared, 'I shall propose an armistice treaty based on the territorial integrity of the [Ottoman] state. If the Admiral won't accept this, I will ask for a cruiser immediately and go straight to London. On arrival, I will have an audience with the King and say "I was an old friend of your father's. I expect you to accept my wishes." Having thus ensured that our proposals are accepted, I'll rescue the state from the catastrophe into which the Unionists have plunged it.' However, he could not leave immediately as he had to pack his clothes. When he was ready, he would leave on the Sultan's yacht, taking with him the secretary of the Greek Patriarch.[25] A year later, the Patriarch was to sever all relations with the Ottoman state and demand that the Ottoman capital should come under Greek rule.

This nonsense confirmed Ahmed İzzet's original estimate

of Damad Ferid's capacity. Loyal to the Sultan as he was, Ahmed İzzet insisted that the cabinet should be free to choose its own chief negotiator. Sultan Vahdettin gave way with bad grace, but insisted that the instructions to the Ottoman delegates should specify that 'the rights of the Sultanate, the Caliphate and of the Ottoman dynasty should be protected',[26] and that the autonomy to be given to some provinces should be administrative and not political. Ahmed İzzet objected that these were matters to be settled in the peace treaty and not in an armistice agreement. Once again the Sultan gave way, but asked that the armistice should at least ensure the safe return of an Ottoman prince who was cut off in Libya.

> **'I will ask for a cruiser immediately and go straight to London. On arrival I will have an audience with the King and say "I was a friend of your father's. I expect you to accept my wishes."'**
> **DAMAD FERID PASHA**

Having warded off – for a short period of time, as it proved – the Sultan's interference, Ahmed İzzet's cabinet chose Rauf, the patriotic naval officer, as chief negotiator. He was told that he could agree to the opening of the Straits and to the reduction in size of the Ottoman army to peacetime strength. However, no Greek warships should be allowed through the Straits, which would be defended by the Ottoman army. British control officers would be allowed until the conclusion of peace, but no Allied forces should land anywhere in the territories which the Ottomans still controlled, and there should be no interference in Ottoman administration. Any conditions incompatible with the honour of the Ottoman state should be rejected. German and Austro-Hungarian troops and officials should be given at least two months to leave the country, but civilians from these countries should be allowed to stay on, if they wished, lest Germany and Austria-Hungary decide to retaliate by expelling from their territories Ottoman students, whose number was estimated at 15–20,000.[27]

The insistence on decent treatment of the Ottomans' German and Austrian allies shows that, in spite of wartime friction between Turks and their German advisers, there was little animosity against them. On the military level, the alliance had worked well. True, the importance of German commanders in the Ottoman war effort was often exaggerated in Britain and France. Their most important help was in communications, staff work and, of course, supplies. The Germans worked hard to maintain and extend Ottoman railways; the Austro-Hungarians provided a motor transport unit on the Caucasian front.[28] In Turkish popular tradition, the Germans stood for precision in everything.

'How do you make a good pilaff?' a German officer asks a Turkish army cook in a well known joke. 'You need enough rice, enough fat, enough water, and cook the rice long enough' the cook replies. But the German wants precise information. 'What do you mean by enough?' he asks. 'It's obvious, Sir,' says the cook, 'enough to make a good pilaff'.

The Germans had their own stories of the happy-go-lucky attitude of Ottoman officers. One day, a German officer was horrified to see that his Ottoman companions were using a map of Gallipoli while fighting the British in Palestine. 'It's the wrong map,' he cried. 'What do you mean by wrong map?' replies the Ottoman. 'It served us well enough all through the campaign in Galicia.' Later these good-natured stories gave way to angrier reminiscences, and today many Turks will tell you that in the First World War, the Germans evacuated their wounded by rail, but left the Turks to die in the desert. This was true, but there were many more Turks than Germans, and the Germans fought in a foreign country while the Turks were, at least theoretically, at home among the Arabs.

The Germans left the Ottoman Empire in good time, but the other conditions on which the Ottoman armistice negotiators were to insist were sacrificed. Rauf and his fellow delegates were acutely aware of the weakness of the Ottoman state and of its urgent need for peace. They did not realise that, late as it was to conclude a separate peace under favourable conditions, there was still room for bargaining. Germany had not yet surrendered and the Allies wanted above all to send their navy through the Turkish Straits in order to cut off German troops in south-eastern Europe and the Caucasus. What is more, they had conflicting ambitions in the Near East. The instructions communicated to Admiral Calthorpe after difficult consultations in London and Paris defined a first bargaining position, but the Admiral was told that he could make concessions, provided the Straits were opened, its fortifications placed under Allied control, the Germans expelled and the Ottoman army demobilised. This Ahmed İzzet's government was, in any case, prepared to concede. But it did not have to agree to peace at any price. There was no domestic pressure for unconditional surrender. In spite of widespread hardships, there were no military mutinies or civil disturbances in the areas under Ottoman control. The Istanbul government did not fear the disaffection of the Sultan's Muslim subjects. What terrified it was the prospect of a rising by local Christians, above all by the numerous Greeks in the capital.

In Turkish eyes, Greece was a Johnny-come-lately in the ranks of the Allies. Greece was still neutral when Allied troops under French command landed in Salonica in October

1916. It was under the protection of the Allies that the Greek prime minister Eleftherios Venizelos formed a provisional government in that city and declared war on Bulgaria and the Central Powers. Greek troops thereafter fought under French command against the Bulgarians and Germans on the Macedonian front, and the Allies made use of Greek territory to prosecute the war with the Ottoman state. But there had been no fighting between Greek and Ottoman troops. Greece was not consulted when Admiral Calthorpe sat down to negotiate an armistice with the Ottoman delegation. However, the Ottoman government was well aware that Greek nationalists, who had found a champion in Venizelos, coveted Constantinople/Istanbul as well as Smyrna/İzmir and the surrounding area. The Turks knew that they had been defeated by the British and not by the Greeks, and resented the idea that the latter should figure among the victorious Allies, particularly in the streets of the imperial capital.

The negotiations between Admiral Calthorpe and Rauf opened on 27 October on board HMS *Agamemnon*, which was anchored in Moudros Bay (Mondros in Turkish), a natural deep-water harbour on the island of Lemnos. The delegations met in the captain's large day cabin, comfortably furnished with Persian rugs, which opened on to a pleasant stern walk. Both sides behaved with impeccable good manners. Calthorpe made some concessions to the Turks. But these concerned conditions on which he had not been instructed to insist. Only one concession was to prove important. Where the Turks had originally been asked to withdraw all their troops from former Tsarist territory in the Caucasus (and north-west Persia, whose neutrality had been violated by both sides during the war), the final text stipulated that 'the remainder [of the Ottoman troops] [is] to be evacuated if requested by the Allies after they have studied the situation'. The Ottoman troops sent by Enver to the Caucasus and Persia had not affected the course of the war. But these fresh divisions, well-armed with weapons from Tsarist arsenals or handed over by the Germans, were to become the nucleus of the Turkish national army when the War of Independence started a year later. A condition in the armistice calling for consultations with the Turkish government to determine the strength and disposition of Ottoman troops which were to maintain internal order after the demobilisation of the bulk of the Ottoman army, allowed Turkish nationalists to keep this military nucleus in order to avert the final catastrophe – the occupation and partition of the whole of Turkey.

The way had been opened for this by the insertion into the text of the armistice of Article 7 which read: 'The Allies have the right to occupy any strategic points in the event of a situation arising which threatens Allied security.' The condition that a threat should arise to justify occupation was included as a concession to the Turks. But it was of no practical effect, since it was the Allies who would decide whether they were threatened. Article 7 meant that the Allies could occupy any part or the whole of Turkey if they were so minded. Rauf had stood out against this clause, but he finally gave way when Calthorpe threatened to break off negotiations. The text of the armistice agreement was signed late in the evening of 30 October.

Immediately after the signing, Calthorpe gave a letter to Rauf promising that only British and French troops would be used to occupy the Straits and that a small number of Turkish soldiers would be allowed to remain when the forts were occupied. This promise was kept. Calthorpe said also that he had passed on the Turkish requests that no Greek warships should sail to Istanbul or İzmir, and that Istanbul should not be occupied unless the Turkish government failed to maintain order there. The request was indeed passed on. But as the Turks were to discover before long, the Allies turned a deaf ear to it.

Calthorpe described the final ceremony in a letter to his wife: 'I had champagne on ice in readiness as I knew that all was going to be well and there was hand-shaking, toasting and polite speeches. Raouf Bey made me a very graceful little speech thanking me for my hospitality and consideration to him as a technical enemy, and he delighted me, and I am sure you, by saying that our twins [whose photograph decorated the cabin] had also taken an important part in this historic event. He said that their cheery smiling faces had been a source of inspiration and encouragement to him in his most difficult and anxious hours. He had often come in and looked at them and they had told him what to do for the cause of humanity. Wasn't that nice!'[29]

Rauf returned to Istanbul on 1 November, convinced that he had won the confidence of the British and had secured the best possible terms. 'Our country's rights and the future of the Sultanate have been wholly saved as a result of the armistice we have concluded', he told journalists, adding: 'First, I discovered that the British are not aiming at the destruction of the Turkish nation. Second, I saw that our country, contrary to what was expected, will not be occupied. I assure you that not a single enemy soldier will disembark in Istanbul ... Yes, the armistice we have concluded is beyond our hopes.'[30]

'I discovered that the British are not aiming at the destruction of our nation ... I assure you that not a single enemy soldier will disembark in Istanbul ... Yes, the armistice we have concluded is beyond our hopes.'

RAUF, CHIEF OTTOMAN DELEGATE AT ARMISTICE NEGOTIATIONS

The Grand Vizier, Ahmed İzzet, was pleased with what Rauf had achieved. Rauf's main concern now was to avoid inter-communal clashes, which would give the Allies grounds for occupying Ottoman territory. He insisted, therefore, that irresponsible statements, likely to increase tension between Muslims and non-Muslims, and in particular between Turks and Greeks, should be avoided. One such statement was attributed to Damad Ferid Pasha who was reported to have said that Ahmed İzzet's government was plotting to massacre Greeks in Istanbul. Damad Ferid was clearly peeved at his exclusion from the armistice negotiations. But his behaviour was symptomatic of the antagonisms which broke out within the Ottoman ruling class. The CUP had made many enemies during its six years in power. There were dissensions within its ranks as well as between it and the ramshackle opposition represented by the Liberal Union, which, disastrously for the fate of the monarchy, Sultan Vahdettin supported.

Immediately on his return, Rauf went to the palace to report on the results of his mission. But Vahdettin pleaded tiredness and said that he would receive him a few days later. When the Sultan finally granted an audience, Rauf took the opportunity to complain about Damad Ferid's behaviour. 'I love Ferid Pasha as a good husband to my sister,' Vahdettin replied deceptively, 'but I do not share his views. I am particularly opposed to his political opinions. That's why we disagree strongly.' Then he blurted out: 'There is a nation out there, which is like a flock of sheep. It needs a shepherd to look after it. I am that shepherd.'[31]

Events were to show that no-one was less qualified to be a shepherd, and that the Sultan shared the illusion of Damad Ferid and the publicists of the Liberal Union that the Allies would allow the Ottoman state to survive and keep its territory if only it made friends with the non-Muslim communities and made room for foreign business, schools and missionaries. This illusion was fed by a nostalgia for the times of Abdülhamid II, when foreigners and local Christians, including the bulk of the Armenians, prospered. A return to the golden age of Abdülhamid, coupled with the abandonment of the late monarch's pan-Islamism which had threatened Britain and France, was the bait that Vahdettin and the Liberal Union offered the Allies. But the Allies were not tempted.

Tevfik Pasha (1845–1936), last Ottoman Grand Vizier, was the son of a general of Crimean origin. He started his civil service career in 1865, and after serving as Ottoman ambassador in various countries, became Foreign Minister in 1895 during the reign of Abdülhamid II. He held office as Grand Vizier briefly after the 1909 counter-revolution, when he tried in vain to prevent the CUP-led troops from fighting their way into the capital. He was then posted as ambassador to London, and was considered sufficiently pro-Allies to be appointed as Grand Vizier shortly after the armistice of 1918. He was unsuccessful in persuading the Allies to moderate their demands at Sèvres. Known as a conciliator, he became Grand Vizier for the third and last time after Damad Ferid's final departure in 1920. Mustafa Kemal did not need his services at the end of the War of Independence, allowing him to live undisturbed in his retirement in Istanbul.

Before this became clear, the Istanbul press, which had been freed from censorship in June 1918, directed its anger at the CUP, including critics of the triumvirate who were now members of the cabinet. The attacks redoubled when the CUP leadership – Enver, Cemal, Talât and a handful of close associates, including the former police chief in the capital – slipped out of Istanbul in the night of 1/2 November on board a German U-boat.[32] The following day they arrived in German-occupied Crimea. None of them was to see Turkey again.

In Istanbul, Ahmed İzzet's cabinet was accused by the opposition of collusion in the flight or, at least, incompetence in failing to prevent it. This gave the Sultan the opportunity to press for the exclusion from the government of former members of the CUP. Rather than comply with what he saw as an abuse of the sovereign's prerogative, Ahmed İzzet submitted his resignation on 11 November 1918 after less than a month in office.

He was succeeded by an even older man, Ahmed Tevfik Pasha, who had been the last Grand Vizier of Sultan Abdülhamid. As he saw monarchies tumble first in Russia, then in Austria-Hungary and Germany, Vahdettin feared betrayal by his own ministers. In the case of Ahmed Tevfik, he thought that he could count, at least, on family loyalty, as the new Grand Vizier's son was courting and was soon to marry Vahdettin's daughter. Thus with a fearful and suspicious Sultan on the throne, yesterday's men – Enver, Cemal and Talât – were replaced by the men of the day before yesterday. It is in their company that Sultan Vahdettin presided over the demise of the Ottoman Empire.

2

Broken Promises

The armistice agreement provided that all hostilities were to cease on 31 October 1918. This was clear enough. But there were clauses in the agreement which were open to wilful misinterpretation. One such clause gave the Allies the right to occupy any strategic points if their security was threatened. Other clauses listed the Arab provinces where any remaining Turkish garrisons were to surrender, and also areas which the Ottoman army had to evacuate. However, the lists were not based on existing administrative divisions. Turkish garrisons were to surrender in Mesopotamia; they had to withdraw from Cilicia. But these regions, named in classical antiquity, had no precise borders.

On 1 November, the British commander in Mesopotamia ordered his troops to occupy Mosul. The local Ottoman commander protested that Mosul was not in Mesopotamia and that Allied security was not threatened. The Grand Vizier, Ahmed İzzet, instructed the Ottoman commander to comply, adding bitterly, 'I fail to understand how the British can use the sophistry of one of their officers to break the word they gave two days ago.'[1] The British occupied Mosul on 8

November. A report written in July 1918 by the oil expert of the Royal Navy, Rear Admiral Sir Edmond Slade, had stressed the importance of British control over the newly discovered oilfield in the province of Mosul.[2] British proconsuls pondering the political future of Mesopotamia as British-Mandated Iraq, believed that the new state would be indefensible without the province of Mosul, which provided a natural northern rampart. A self-denying interpretation of the armistice agreement was not going to stand in their way.

On the borders of Syria, Mustafa Kemal ordered his troops to resist the British who wanted to occupy the port of Alexandretta (İskenderun) soon after the armistice was signed. Once again, the Istanbul government ordered him to give way. Alexandretta was the port of Aleppo, and its facilities were needed to supply British troops, which had occupied northern Syria and were about to cede it to the French. On 25 November a French officer arrived in Adana, the main Turkish city south of the Taurus range at the centre of the Cilician plain, and told the Ottoman governor that as French troops intended to occupy the area, Turkish troops should be withdrawn immediately. The French army duly arrived on 21 December, accompanied by Armenian auxiliaries. Armenians who had been expelled in 1915 began to return.[3] It was only at this point that Turkish nationalist resistance became a threat to Allied security.

Mustafa Kemal had by then left Adana. After the Ottoman war ministry had abolished his command, he made his way to Istanbul where he arrived on 13 November. When he stepped off the train, he saw 55 Allied warships steam into the harbour and prepare to anchor off the Sultan's palace at Dolmabahçe.[4] *Just as they have come, so too will they go*, he is reported to have said.[5] Soon afterwards, Vahdettin moved to Abdülhamid's old palace at Yıldız, up the hill from Dolmabahçe.

Its seclusion suited the new Sultan's secretive and suspicious nature, which he shared with his long-reigning elder brother, Abdülhamid. But while Abdülhamid had an intelligent grasp of world affairs and knew how to safeguard his dominions, Vahdettin lived in a fog of misapprehensions. The heir apparent, Vahdettin's cousin and discreet critic Abdülmecid, took up residence in Dolmabahçe with its panoramic view of the Allied warships.

'Just as they have come, so too they will go.'
MUSTAFA KEMAL, SPEAKING OF ALLIED WARSHIPS IN ISTANBUL

An initial group of British officers had arrived in Istanbul on 7 November on board an Ottoman torpedo-boat. They were met by a crowd shouting 'Long live the Allies.' As soon as the armistice was announced, Christians and foreigners in the capital put out Allied flags in their neighbourhoods. Greek flags were particularly prominent, reflecting the strength of the Greek community. The Muslims resented what they saw as the impertinence of the Sultan's Greek subjects. Inter-communal friction grew, but neither then nor in the subsequent four years which were to pass before Istanbul came once again under Turkish rule, were there any clashes between the religious communities, let alone a rising by local Greeks. Allied security was not threatened. Nevertheless, Istanbul was placed under informal Allied occupation. Admiral Calthorpe became Allied High Commissioner, governing with the help of British, French and Italian commissioners. British troops which disembarked on 13 November were joined by a French brigade, sent by rail from Salonica, and then by an Italian contingent. Most galling of all to the Turks, the Greek Patriarchate, the office of the Greek High Commissioner and other Greek premises were guarded by Greek soldiers.

The word 'occupation' was studiously avoided, but Allied

control officers were attached to all Ottoman ministries and police. Public buildings and private residences were requisitioned to accommodate them. The Allies had their own courts, police and detention centres, as well as competing and overlapping intelligence services, employing a host of local informers. At one time the French alone had four separate intelligence agencies, all scrambling to supply political information. Allied intelligence officers divided their attention between the CUP underground, to which they attributed the rise in Turkish nationalist feeling, and Bolshevik agents, whom they suspected of colluding with Turkish nationalists to thwart Allied designs.

As Allied controls multiplied, so public security deteriorated in the capital. A French journalist, who had known Istanbul before the War, wrote: 'Murders, burglaries and kidnappings have never been so frequent and gone so generally unpunished. It is easy to see why. Instead, or rather on top, of the Turkish police there is now an inter-allied police, whose commander is British and whose officers are British, Italian and French, roughly in equal numbers. The job of fighting crime has thus been entrusted to fine fellows, who may be professionally well qualified, but who know nothing of the country, its geography or the languages and customs of its inhabitants. When two British officers stopped the motor car of the Grand Vizier for speeding and arrested its occupant, gossip in the European quarter had it that it was a devilishly clever plot to lay hands on documents in the car. My guess is though that the British policemen who arrested Tevfik Paşa did not know him, and that had they recognised him they would have let him through, as they would have let through Mr Lloyd George in similar circumstances.'[6]

The arrival in November 1920 of tens of thousands of

White Russians, the remnants of the forces defeated by the Bolsheviks in the Russian Civil War, compounded the confusion. The Russians were destitute. So too were thousands of Muslim refugees from the war zones. There were Armenian orphans whose families had perished during the deportations, and Greeks who sought their fortune in the capital. Western aid agencies, chief among them the American Near Eastern Relief, eased the lot of Christians. The Muslims, who filled the courtyards of mosques and other public buildings, had to rely on the charity of their compatriots. The Ottoman treasury was bankrupt and had to solicit foreign loans in order to pay the salaries of the military and the civil service which were the main employers of educated Turks.

General Sir (later Field Marshal Lord) Edmund Allenby (1861–1936), last great British commander of horsed cavalry, saw service in the Boer War and on the Western Front in the First World War, before being put in command in June 1917 of the Egyptian Expeditionary Force, which had made no progress against Ottoman troops for over two years. In a daring campaign of rapid movement, he captured the Ottoman fortress of Gaza and entered Jerusalem – on foot as a sign of respect – in December 1917. After regrouping his troops, he shattered the remaining Ottoman forces, commanded by Mustafa Kemal, on the plain of Megiddo in northern Palestine. The Allenby bridge over the river Jordan perpetuates his memory. After the war, Allenby served as High Commissioner in Egypt, which was recognised as a sovereign state in 1922.

White Russian women found employment as hostesses in bars and night clubs. Russian theosophists, George Gurdjieff (who became notorious as the guru of the dying Katherine Mansfield) and Peter Ouspensky, made their appearance before moving on to Paris. Table-tapping and other forms of mumbo-jumbo popular in *fin de siècle* St Petersburg brought together locals and Allied officers, who were also fascinated by Whirling Dervishes and other quaint Oriental spectacles.

General Allenby arrived in Istanbul on 7 February 1919 and presented a list of demands to the Ottoman government. The French, convinced as ever, that the British were trying to elbow them out, sent General Franchet d'Esperey, the commander of the Salonica-based Army of the Orient. He made a triumphal entry on 8 February, mounted on a white charger. Local Christians were delirious with pleasure. But far from safeguarding them – let alone making them top dog in a diverse city – Allied occupation endangered their survival in the face of Turkish resentment. Like the British, the French tried at first to build up the Sultan as a useful puppet. Addressing students at the Imperial Lycée, which educated the Turkish ruling class in French culture, Franchet d'Esperey described Vahdettin as 'the best and most enlightened of Sultans', who was labouring to bring peace and security to his country.[7] The Turks, treated like colonial native subjects of the Emperor of Annam, were not impressed. But they noted the rivalry between the Allies and turned it to their advantage.

General (later Marshal) **Louis Franchet d'Esperey (1856–1942) first saw service in North Africa, where he was born. Having failed to hold the Chemin des Dames against the German offensive of May 1918 on the Western Front, he was appointed commander in May 1918 of the Army of the Orient, the multi-national Allied force assembled in Salonica. He led it to victory against the Bulgarians four months later, and pushing rapidly to the Danube, scattered the remaining German forces in south-eastern Europe, and forced Hungary to surrender.**

First, however, the Turks had to deal with demands the Allies had made earlier that CUP leaders should be arrested and Ottoman war criminals should be tried. As parliament, in which the CUP still had a presence, resisted Allied pressure, Vahdettin dissolved it on 21 December. On 13 January Tevfik Pasha was asked to form a new and more compliant government. But this too failed to satisfy the Allies or the Sultan who wanted to have a free hand to steer the country into the safe harbour of British protection. Tevfik Pasha was forced to resign and on 4 March 1919, the Sultan's brother-in-law, and first choice all along, Damad Ferid became Grand Vizier. The Allies, and particularly the British, thought they had found their man.

Damad Ferid wasted no time in trying to satisfy their expectations. On 8 March a court martial was set up to try war criminals, including the CUP leadership which, in the words of the new Minister of the Interior, was responsible 'for the murder of 800,000 Armenians, the deportation of 400,000 Greeks and the deaths of four million Turks'.[8]

Leading Unionists, including opponents of the leadership, and Turkish nationalists, generally, both military and civilian, were arrested. Journalists, who had fallen foul of the CUP, clamoured for revenge. 'These men are not worthy of the gallows,' wrote one opponent of the CUP, 'their heads should be wrenched off and exhibited for days on chopping-blocks as a warning to the public.'[9] The violence of the language of pro-Allied journalists during the occupation has bequeathed the expression 'armistice press', used to this day in Turkey to stigmatise publications deemed to damage the national interest.

On 10 April, an Ottoman civil servant who had been deputy governor of a province in central Anatolia during the Armenian deportations was hanged in a public square. His funeral caused such an explosion of nationalist anger that Damad Ferid's government desisted from further executions and, fearing an attempt to free the arrested nationalists, asked the British High Commissioner to deport them to Malta. As the trial of the CUP leadership dragged on, the composition of the Istanbul court martial changed repeatedly. Finally, the

CUP leaders who had fled the country were sentenced to death *in absentia*, but the verdict made it clear that all this meant was that they would be re-tried if they ever returned.

The value of the testimony laid before the court is hotly disputed. Advocates of the claim that the deportations put into effect a project by the CUP government to destroy the Armenians as an ethnic community and should, therefore, be condemned as an act of genocide, cite the text of the indictment and extracts from witnesses' statements which were published in the official gazette of the Ottoman government in Istanbul. Their opponents dismiss the courts martial as tools of victors' justice, and point to shortcomings in their conduct, to the loss of documentation, and to instances of forgery by Armenian nationalists. They also cite the statement by Admiral Sir John de Robeck, who replaced Admiral Calthorpe in 1919 as Commander-in-Chief Mediterranean and British High Commissioner in Istanbul, that the trials were a dead failure and that 'their findings cannot be held of any account at all'.[10] The British authorities subsequently decided not to put on trial any of the leading Turkish nationalists, associated with the CUP, whom they held in detention in Malta.

Sultan Vahdettin and his brother-in-law, the Grand Vizier, Damad Ferid, deluded themselves into thinking that by bending to the demands of the Allies they would secure the territory still controlled by the Ottoman army at the end of the hostilities. The British, in particular, did not help the men who had volunteered to be their puppets. Admiral Calthorpe, the first British High Commissioner in Istanbul, declared 'it has been our consistent attitude to show no kind of favour whatsoever to any Turk ...' He added for good measure: 'All interchange of hospitality and comity has been rigorously forbidden.'[11] No wonder that Rauf, who had negotiated the armistice, and believed that he had won Calthorpe's trust and friendship, resigned his commission in the Ottoman navy and warned Damad Ferid that his policy would cause a rebellion.[12]

Calthorpe may have been needlessly provocative, but he was not responsible for policy. He had negotiated the armistice on behalf of all the Allies. Then as British High Commissioner, he chaired the meetings of Allied representatives in the Ottoman capital. The Allies had conflicting designs in Turkey. They were agreed on partitioning the country, but they disagreed on the distribution of spoils.

'It has been our consistent attitude to show no kind of favour whatsoever to any Turk ... All interchange of hospitality and comity has been rigorously forbidden.'

LORD CALTHORPE, BRITISH HIGH COMMISSIONER IN ISTANBUL

Britain's traditional preoccupation was with the safety of the route to India. Having achieved political control over Egypt and the shores of the Persian Gulf before the War, British governments were not at first keen to rule other Ottoman territories. But as British armies moved north into Palestine, Syria and Mesopotamia, the appetite grew for a more permanent presence in these lands.

Tsarist Russia had two traditional ambitions: to gain Constantinople and with it control of the sea lanes in and out of the Black Sea and to add to its conquest of the Caucasus. France had extensive investments in the Ottoman Empire and wished to buttress them with direct political control. In addition, it saw itself as the protector of Catholics, including Uniates (members of indigenous Christian communities which accepted the primacy of the Pope), particularly in Lebanon, where it had become the patron of the Maronite (Uniate) community. Italy, having wrested from the Ottomans

Tripolitania, Cyrenaica and the Dodecanese Islands on the eve of the First World War, wanted to be rewarded with a zone of influence in Anatolia.

At the same time, the Allies sought to protect themselves against each other. Britain looked for buffer zones between its possessions and those of its ally, and rival, Russia. The French were convinced that the British wanted to reduce to the minimum their political influence in the Near East, and the Italians had a well-founded suspicion that their ambitions did not enjoy the full-hearted support of their allies. As the war progressed, the Allies concluded and then revised agreements in order to reconcile their conflicting demands.

It was the British attempt in 1915 to force a passage through the Straits in order to open up a supply route to the hard-pressed Russian armies that aroused the Russians' fears that they might be done out of Constantinople, if the British got there first. This gave rise to the first partition agreement in March 1915 between Britain and Russia, to which France gave its assent the following month. The Russians were promised Constantinople. What prompted Britain and France to enter unwillingly into this commitment was the fear that, if they did not, Russia might change sides in the war.[13] Trust was in short supply in inter-Allied relations.

It was Britain which called the shots in the intricate negotiations on the disposal of Ottoman lands; and Britain's Near Eastern policy had been taken over by a bunch of young Conservatives, the 'Neocons' of the time, who were in cahoots with Liberal imperialists. The most active of these was Sir Mark Sykes, a Catholic baronet, heir to large estates on Humberside. As a young man, he had travelled in the Ottoman Empire soon after power had been seized by the Young Turks, to whom he took an instant dislike. In temperament he was a Young Turk himself, a young ambitious amateur. But he was well-born, and the Young Turks were in his eyes a bunch of parvenus manipulated by Jews and Freemasons. Sykes's obsession with the Jews, whose hand he saw in every twist and turn of politics, had been fed by another Catholic, the Irishman Gerald Fitzmaurice, who, as Chief Dragoman (interpreter, the title given to the official who acted as intermediary between a foreign embassy and local authorities), was the local expert at the British embassy in Constantinople. Sir Aubrey Herbert, a friend of Mark Sykes and, like him, a young conservative MP, thought Fitzmaurice 'cunning as a weasel and as savage'.[14] But cunning as he was, the Chief Dragoman did not understand that the Young Turks were first and foremost Turkish nationalists, and not the instruments of a Judaeo-Masonic conspiracy.

The British government had a better expert in the person of Brigadier Sir Wyndham Deedes, a squire from Kent (and uncle of the distinguished journalist and Conservative junior minister Bill Deedes). Herbert and Deedes saw themselves as pro-Turkish, but after the CUP had thrown in its lot with the Germans, their knowledge of Turkey was deployed to no good purpose in the failed Gallipoli expedition, while Sykes became the leading member of a government committee set up in London to plan the future governance of the Near East. After the armistice, Deedes was posted to Istanbul, but his advice was disregarded.

Wild exaggerations of the power of world Jewry had a paradoxical consequence in the issue of the Balfour Declaration on 2 November 1917, promising British support for 'the establishment in Palestine of a national home for the Jewish people'. For if the Jews were so powerful, it was essential to detach them from the Germans and enlist them for the Allied cause. In the words of the distinguished Middle Eastern scholar, Elie Kedourie, 'it may well be that such fictions helped to persuade the British government to fall for and take up Zionism: Clio is indeed an ironic muse.'[15]

Sykes and Deedes became Zionists. Their feelings were shared by Lloyd George, whose Christian Zionism was rooted in the Biblical inspiration of Welsh Nonconformist Protestants. The First Lord of the Admiralty, Winston Churchill, who was a member of the Liberal Party at that time, having started as a Conservative, and who was later to re-cross the floor and rejoin the Tories, was also sympathetic to the Zionist project. Churchill, who throughout his life demonstrated the truth of the saying that consistency is the mark of a small mind, had converted from a pro-Turkish to a virulently anti-Turkish stance (before becoming much more sensible about Turkey in 1923 after his policy had been thwarted by the Turks).

Not surprisingly, the Turks had few friends in London during the First World War. Lord Curzon, former Viceroy of India and a leading member of the War Cabinet after 1916, who believed that he had mastered 'the art of getting on with Orientals',[16] advocated firmness in dealing with them. His aversion to the Turks (and to foreigners generally) was shared by many British diplomats, including the young diplomat, snobbish recorder of contemporary events and political maverick, Harold Nicolson, the son of Sir Arthur Nicolson, the Permanent Under-Secretary at the Foreign Office. But the most determined – and least knowledgeable – opponent of the Turks was Lloyd George. His Nonconformist background predisposed him to follow in the steps of Gladstone who had taken up the cause of Christian communities in the Ottoman Empire and wished to see the Turks driven out of Europe 'bag and baggage'.

Lloyd George's support for Greek nationalist ambitions at the expense of Turkey can be traced back to the Balkan War in 1912 when, as a practising solicitor in London, he became friends with a Greek expatriate solicitor (and political intriguer) John Stavridi. At a dinner at 11 Downing Street, at which both Stavridi and Lloyd George were present, Britain's future wartime leader ordered champagne and proposed the following toast: 'I drink to the [Balkan] allies, the representative of one of whom we have here tonight, and may the Turk be turned out of Europe and sent to ... where he came from.'[17] Stavridi was in contact with the Greek nationalist leader, the Cretan lawyer Eleftherios Venizelos, who first became prime minister in 1910, and who was to return to power in Athens at the end of the War after heading the breakaway pro-Allied government in Salonica. Lloyd George met Venizelos and fell under his spell. Venizelos was ably seconded by the wealthy and well-connected Greek community of expatriate merchants and shipowners who canvassed support for the Great Project (literally 'Great Idea', *Meghali Idhea*, a translation of the French journalistic cliché, *la grande idée du 19ème siècle*, when there were many such grand projects) – the recreation of the Byzantine Empire.

However, Greek ambitions did not figure in the original partition plans. The inter-Allied agreement ceding Istanbul to the Russians was followed by the plan drawn up in London by Mark Sykes and a French representative, François Georges Picot, in May 1916, after the failure of the Gallipoli operation. This partition plan, with which first Russia and then Italy were associated, divided all Ottoman territories outside a small area in central and northern Anatolia between the four Principal Allies. Russia, having already been promised Istanbul, was to acquire Turkey's Black Sea coast up to a point west of Trabzon (Trebizond) and a large tract of eastern Anatolia. The gains of the Western Allies would come in two forms: areas which were to be placed under their direct control and zones of influence. The Italians were to get western and south-western Anatolia, including İzmir and Antalya, as their fief and a further area north of İzmir as a zone of influence. The French were promised direct control of the coastal area from northern Palestine through to Cilicia, and a chunk of territory in inland Anatolia. In addition, their zone of influence was to extend from the Syrian coast eastwards as far as, and including, Mosul. They would thus separate Russian acquisitions from British gains, which included direct control of what is now southern Iraq, and a zone of influence from the River Jordan eastwards to the Persian frontier. The Holy Land was to become an international zone.

The Sykes-Picot agreement assumed its final form in April 1917 after a meeting of British, French and Italian leaders at St Jean de Maurienne on the Franco-Italian border. Russia, which was in turmoil after the revolution in February that year and the fall of the monarchy, was not represented. In any case, all previous concessions to the Russians were cancelled when the Bolsheviks seized power in November and then negotiated a separate peace with Germany in March 1918. The Bolsheviks for their part repudiated all the secret treaties concluded by their predecessors and, to the embarrassment of the Western Allies, published their texts, which thus became known to the Turks. However this knowledge does not seem to have affected the expectations of the Ottoman representatives who negotiated the armistice at the end of October that year. In their minds, wartime arrangements had been superseded by President Wilson's repudiation of secret treaties and his promise to satisfy legitimate national rights through open diplomacy. But as far as the Allies were concerned, the Sykes-Picot partition plan, as modified at St Jean de Maurienne and then by the collapse of Tsarist Russia, was, at least in theory, still the basis of a Near Eastern settlement.

Nevertheless, the spirit of Woodrow Wilson brooded over the Peace Conference which opened in Versailles in January 1919. Its first product was the Covenant of the League of Nations which was approved the following month. Article 22 of the Covenant proclaimed in self-righteous terms: 'To those colonies and territories which, as a consequence of the late war, have ceased to be under the sovereignty of the States which formerly governed them and which are inhabited by peoples not yet ready to stand by themselves under the strenuous conditions of the modern world, there should be applied the principle that the well-being and development of such peoples form a sacred trust of civilisation … The best method of giving practical effect to this principle is that the tutelage of such peoples should be entrusted to advanced nations who by reason of their resources, their experience or their geographical position can best undertake this responsibility, and who are willing to accept it, and that this tutelage should be exercised by them as Mandatories on behalf of the League … Certain communities formerly belonging to the Turkish Empire have reached a stage of development where their existence as independent nations can be provisionally recognised subject to the rendering of administrative advice and assistance by a Mandatory until such time as they are able to stand alone. The wishes of these communities must be a principal consideration in the selection of a Mandatory.'

These admirable sentiments were immediately disregarded, as no one asked the Arabs whether they preferred the British or the French to rule over them as Mandatories. More to the point, it was unclear whether Turks themselves were to be numbered among the communities 'formerly belonging to the Turkish Empire'. The Turks, it will be remembered, had been promised 'secure sovereignty' in 'the Turkish portions of the Ottoman Empire' under Woodrow Wilson's Twelfth Point, while other Turkish-ruled nationalities were promised only 'security of life' and 'autonomous development'. No wonder that when an American mission under General Harbord was sent to Anatolia to determine the feelings of its inhabitants, it was greeted with banners proclaiming '*Vive l'Article 12 des principes de Wilson*'.[18] Nor is it surprising that a Society for Wilson's Principles was formed in Istanbul in 1919 by a number of educated Turkish patriots. The best known among them was the feminist writer Halide Edip, who was born in Salonica (as was her husband, Dr Adnan, a liberal Turkish nationalist, who later took the surname Adıvar).

However, apart from inspiring the idea of Mandates, and, as a result, injecting a considerable measure of hypocrisy into the intrigues of the European Allies over their respective shares of Ottoman territory, the United States had little to do with the peace settlement which eventually emerged in the Near East. Lloyd George did his best to use the Americans against the French, then the Italians and finally against the Bolsheviks and Turkish nationalists. An American Mandate over Palestine was briefly discussed, and as quickly abandoned. Then Lloyd George toyed with the idea of an American Mandate over Constantinople, before deciding to concentrate his efforts on persuading the Americans to accept a Mandate over the proposed independent state of Armenia. But in spite of the strength of the Armenian lobby in the United States, Congress stood out against any foreign entanglements. With

America therefore largely off-stage, Britain, France and Italy were left to decide the fate of Turkey among themselves.

Britain and France agreed eventually on their shares of the Arab provinces of the Ottoman Empire – Britain acquiring Mandates over Palestine, Transjordan and Iraq, and France over Syria and Lebanon. But in the tussle over the Turkish heartland, Lloyd George paid the price of his notorious deviousness. His attempt to out-manoeuvre France and Italy impelled both countries to break ranks and make their own terms with Turkish nationalists. But at first, the pretence of a common Allied policy was maintained.

On 1 December 1918, a month after the conclusion of the Turkish armistice, the British and French wartime leaders, Lloyd George and Georges Clemenceau, met in London. In order to win British support for harsh treatment of Germany, Clemenceau promised Lloyd George to give up Mosul and to raise no objection to British control over Palestine. But this was not enough for Lloyd George. He tried to push the French out of Syria too by exaggerating the contribution to victory of the Bedouins payrolled by Britain to serve in the Hashemite rebellion against Ottoman rule. Although he admitted in private that the Arab contribution to the conquest of Palestine and Syria 'was almost insignificant',[19] he allowed the Hashemite Prince Feisal to take over civil government in Damascus. However, Britain's rapidly diminishing resources forced the withdrawal of British occupation troops from Syria. They were replaced by the French who had established their headquarters in Beirut. Feisal was left to make his own terms with them. His position soon became untenable as local Syrians were as eager as the French to get rid of him and of his hungry Bedouins. Finally the British repaid their much exaggerated debt to the Hashemites by installing Feisal as King of Iraq, whose disparate communities were forced to accept him against their will, while his brother Abdullah, was made Emir (Prince) of Transjordan, where the Bedouins had always roamed.

The French repaid in kind Lloyd George's transparent manoeuvre to wriggle out of the promises made under the Sykes-Picot agreement. Sir Mark Sykes, its British author, was not available to defend it: he died of influenza in Paris in February 1919, just as his work was being undone. (His body was exhumed in 2008 to provide a sample of the DNA of the Spanish 'flu virus.) What the French saw as British betrayal in Syria led inevitably to French betrayal of their British allies in Turkey. But before that happened, the two Allies betrayed their third partner, Italy. They did so with the help of Woodrow Wilson, who was determined that the Italians should not have İzmir. That, in his eyes, would be a display of imperialism which he had promised to banish from the world.

Italian troops had landed in Antalya, on Turkey's Mediterranean coast, in January 1919 and had begun to fan out north and west. The Turkish population did not resist them. The occupied areas had faced starvation and the lifting of the Allied blockade and the arrival of supplies brought welcome relief. But there was a more important reason for Turkish acquiescence. Many Turks, including leading nationalists, felt that occupation by 'civilised' European powers would be temporary. Mustafa Kemal was not alone in claiming to have foreseen that the Western Allies would pack up and go. Another Turkish nationalist commander, General Kâzım Karabekir, wrote in his memoirs that he had always argued that the Turks would have to fight not the Western Allies, but only the Greeks and the Armenians who wished to oust them from their homeland. The thought of their former subjects

Turkey, Greece and Bulgaria 1912–1923

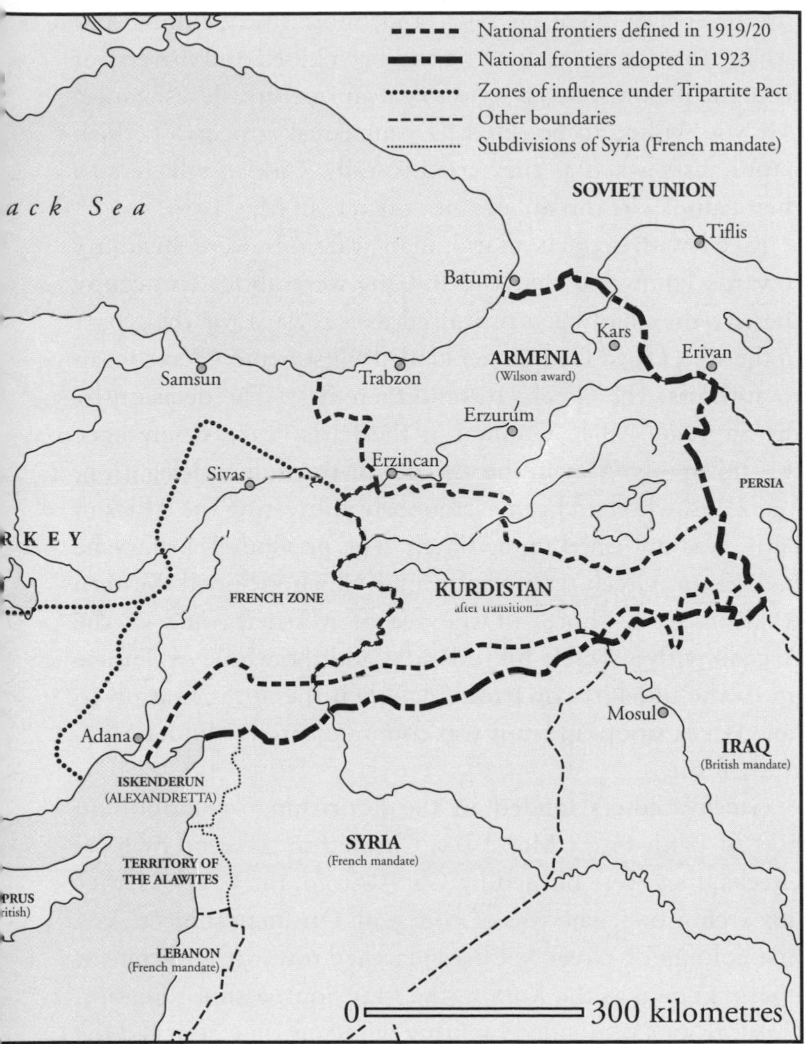
National frontiers defined in 1919/20
National frontiers adopted in 1923
Zones of influence under Tripartite Pact
Other boundaries
Subdivisions of Syria (French mandate)
SOVIET UNION
ack Sea
Tiflis
Batumi
Kars
Erivan
ARMENIA
(Wilson award)
Samsun
Trabzon
Erzurum
Erzincan
Sivas
PERSIA
RKEY
FRENCH ZONE
KURDISTAN
after transition
Mosul
IRAQ
(British mandate)
Adana
ISKENDERUN
(ALEXANDRETTA)
SYRIA
(French mandate)
TERRITORY OF
THE ALAWITES
PRUS
ritish)
LEBANON
(French mandate)
0
300 kilometres

lording it over them, at best, and, more likely, killing and driving them out, as Muslims had been killed and driven out from the Balkans, was bound to galvanize Turkish resistance. 'Are you willing to be ruled by your Greek grocer?' Turkish nationalists asked as they tried to rally Turkish villagers to their cause. The threat became concrete in May 1919.

Faced with reports that Italian warships were steaming towards İzmir and that the Italians were about to occupy the city they had been promised as a reward for their part in the war, Lloyd George persuaded Wilson and Clemenceau to authorise the Greeks to land there first. The decision by the Supreme Allied Council at the Paris Peace Conference was taken on 6 May in the absence of the Italian delegation. Venizelos, who had been assiduously cultivating the Allies in Paris, was informed immediately. The previous February he had set out Greek territorial claims which included Western Anatolia – the shores of the Sea of Marmara and of the Aegean with a sizable hinterland – and the whole of Thrace up to the outskirts of Istanbul. When the authorisation to land Greek troops in İzmir was communicated to him, he was ready for it.

Greek soldiers landed in the flourishing cosmopolitan port of İzmir on 15 May 1919. Cheered to the echo by local Greeks, they were blessed by Chrysostom, the Greek Orthodox archbishop, who was of course an Ottoman subject. As a first column of Greek soldiers marched towards government house, known as the *Konak* (the Mansion), a shot rang out. Greek troops responded by firing wildly as they attacked the barracks of the small Turkish garrison, which had no option but to surrender. Captured Turkish soldiers were kicked and bayoneted. Then a mob of the local Greek underclass looted the main Turkish neighbourhood, maltreating its inhabitants.

Worse was to follow as Greek troops advanced inland. The town of Aydın (after which the province of İzmir was named) was destroyed, as a weak contingent of the Greek soldiers was driven out by a local Turkish resistance band, which ransacked the Greek quarter, and then the Greeks returned in force and set fire to the Turkish quarter.

The Allies, who had tried to justify the Greek occupation on the grounds that it would ensure the security of the local population, were shocked into appointing a commission of enquiry under the American High Commissioner in Istanbul, Admiral Bristol. Its findings were highly unfavourable to the Greeks, whom it held responsible for the incidents which had followed the landings. More importantly, it noted that the occupation had 'assumed all the forms of an annexation', and recommended that the Greek troops should be replaced by Allied troops under the authority of the Supreme Allied Commander in Asia Minor. When the report of the commission was considered by the Supreme Allied Council in Paris on 9 November 1919, Clemenceau questioned the desirability of the Greek presence in Asia Minor. His doubts were ignored. But they presaged a division in the ranks of the Allies.

Venizelos tried to hasten a peace settlement with Turkey before he was left alone to face growing Turkish resistance. But the Allies had other priorities. As a temporary measure, at the suggestion of General George Milne, the commander of British forces in Turkey, a line was drawn beyond which Greek troops were not to advance. The Milne Line, as it came to be known, also served to prevent friction between Greek forces and Italian troops who had landed south of İzmir and held the small port, known at the time in the West by its Italian name of Scala Nova,[20] and much better known to millions of tourists today as the flourishing resort of Kuşadası, near the ruins of ancient Ephesus. An open clash between Greeks and Italians was indeed avoided, but the latter, having lost the prize of İzmir, retaliated by being the first of the Principal Allies to offer discreet help to Turkish nationalists. They were allowed to use the facilities of Scala Nova to enter and leave the country, and to obtain military equipment, as the Italians looked the other way. Count Carlo Sforza, who had served as an Italian diplomat in Istanbul and became Foreign Minister in 1920 (refusing two years later to serve the Fascists after Mussolini's march on Rome), was critical of Lloyd George's policy of supporting (and, at times, egging on) the Greeks in their expansionist ambitions. During the five months he spent in Istanbul between December 1918 and May 1919, Mustafa Kemal was promised Italian protection should the British try to arrest him. The intermediary was Mme Corinne Lütfi, the Italian widow of an Ottoman naval officer, who was young Mustafa Kemal's intimate friend and mentor in Western manners.

Lloyd George's enthusiasm for Greek ambitions could not be curbed. But the number of doubters grew, particularly as in one Allied country after another wartime leaders lost power. In France Clemenceau gave way to January 1920 to Alexandre Millerand. Millerand explored the possibility of a bargain with Turkish nationalists, which would leave the French in secure possession of Syria and Lebanon. In Italy, the prime minister Vittorio Emanuele Orlando, who had brought Italy into the war on the side of the Allies, was beset by labour unrest on one side and nationalist fury whipped up by Mussolini's Blackshirts on the other. He resigned on 19 June 1919, nine days before the signature of the Treaty at Versailles. In the United States, Wilson suffered a stroke in October 1919. The following March, the Senate failed to ratify the Covenant of the League of Nations. Later that year the rise of isolationist sentiment was demonstrated by the election to the presidency of the Republican candidate Warren Harding. Wilson had to console himself with the Nobel Peace Prize and the role of a sage and prophet.

In London, the Secretary of State for India, Edwin Montagu, argued that Lloyd George's hostility to the Turks risked the loyalty of Britain's Muslim subjects in India. Lloyd George was not deterred, but fewer and fewer people came to share his vision of a Greater Greece replacing Turkey as the bulwark of security in the Near East. As the Allies tried to hammer out a common position on the Turkish peace treaty they became progressively less capable of enforcing it. The First World War had bled them dry and their peoples were clamouring for immediate relief. Lack of resources and domestic unrest forced the pace of demobilisation.

At the same time, Woodrow Wilson's rhetoric had affected public opinion, and the self-confidence of empire-builders was shaken. A Government of India Act, passed in 1919, in spite of Winston Churchill's fierce opposition, transferred some functions of provincial administration to Indian ministers responsible to an Indian electorate. It was Edwin Montagu's greatest achievement before his disagreement with Lloyd George's Turkish policy forced him to resign in 1922. It could be argued that the Indians were rewarded for their loyal contribution to the Allied victory, and that the Turks deserved no reward. But Hindus as well as Indian Muslims thought otherwise. A *Khilafat* (Caliphate Movement) had been launched by Indian Muslims before the outbreak of the War in defence of Ottoman Muslims. It counted among its supporters Abul Kalam Azad, destined to become first president of independent India after the Second World War. When the First World War ended, the *Khilafat* joined forces with Mahatma Gandhi's non-cooperation campaign for Indian freedom. The alliance of Muslims and Hindus proved short-lived, but it worried the British government.

The denial of national rights to the Turks was proving hard to justify at a time when these rights were graciously conceded to Latvians, Lithuanians and others who had made no contribution to the Allied victory, and when the Bolsheviks made specious promises of national rights to all and sundry from Buriat-Mongols on the shores of Lake Baykal in distant Siberia to Kabardino-Balkars and other obscure tribes in the mountains of the Caucasus. Lloyd George claimed that he was working for the liberation of oppressed Greeks and Armenians. But what about the Turks, or as British politicians, wedded to national stereotypes, preferred to say, 'the Turk'? However inconvenient it was for Lloyd George, 'the Turk' too had raised the banner of national rights and liberation.

3

Turks Fight for their Rights

Traffic swirls past the statue of Hasan Tahsin in Konak (Government House) Square on the impressive newly-rebuilt waterfront of İzmir. Hasan Tahsin was the pseudonym of the journalist who shot dead the standard-bearer of the first Greek detachment of occupation troops in İzmir on 15 May 1919 (and was himself killed soon afterwards). The statue, which shows Hasan Tahsin raising the Turkish flag (rather than shooting at the Greek flag), is known as the monument to The First Shot in the Turkish War of Independence. Few passers-by know that Hasan Tahsin was a member of the CUP Special Organisation, set up to conduct unconventional warfare. Hasan Tahsin's first shot had been less successful: in Bucharest in October 1914, he shot but failed to kill Noel Buxton and his brother Charles, two prominent British liberals associated with the Balkan Committee in London, who had championed Slav Macedonians against the Turks in the opening years of the 20th century and then tried in vain to enlist Bulgaria in the ranks of the Allies.

However, the first organised resistance to the Greek occupation took place not in İzmir city on 15 May 1919, but a fortnight later, on 29 May, in the seaside town of Ayvalık, further north along the eastern shore of the Aegean. Ayvalık was at the time inhabited largely by Greeks (and was then, as now, famous for its olive-oil presses, rather than for the quince trees which gave the town its name). On that day, Lieutenant Colonel Ali (Çetinkaya) ordered his regiment, quartered in the town, to open fire on the Greek troops which moved in to occupy the area. The Greek landing was not thwarted, and Çetinkaya's regiment retreated to the interior. It had little choice in the matter. As a result of demobilisation and desertions, the regiment numbered only 150 men armed with two machine guns. The whole area in and around İzmir, which the Greeks occupied, had been held by 4,400 Turkish soldiers commanded by 143 officers.

Hasan Tahsin, a civilian, and Ali Çetinkaya, a soldier, had in common that they were both active members of the CUP. Çetinkaya survived the war and had a colourful career. Elected member of the Turkish National Assembly, in 1925 he shot dead a fellow-MP, Halid Pasha (known as Mad Halid), a general who had distinguished himself against the Armenians on the eastern front, and later became an outspoken critic of Mustafa Kemal. The following year Çetinkaya presided over the notorious Independence Tribunal (the revolutionary court), which sentenced to death the prominent Young Turk politician Cavid Bey, Ottoman Finance Minister during the First World War, who was unjustly accused of being an organiser of the plot to kill Mustafa Kemal. Today Çetinkaya is commemorated less controversially by the university which bears his name in his native town of Afyonkarahisar in western Anatolia, the first town to be regained by the Turkish army which drove out the Greeks in 1922.

The political trials and executions in 1926, which sealed

the break between Mustafa Kemal and the CUP, have overshadowed the important part played by the CUP in organising early Turkish nationalist resistance after the armistice of Mudros. As recent research shows, the CUP leadership had laid plans for resistance in Anatolia in anticipation of defeat in the First World War. But although most of Turkey's nationalist leaders after the war had been active members of the CUP, they had another, and more important common bond. Most of them were professional soldiers who, as front-line commanders, had personal experience of the deficiencies of Enver's leadership during the war and were well aware of the downside of the alliance with Germany. The CUP had been the standard-bearer of Turkish nationalism which had arisen as a response to the claims of other national communities in the Ottoman Empire. When the defeated CUP leaders fled the country discredited in November 1918, the standard passed to other hands – the hands of their erstwhile companions and rivals.

The nationalist officers, who organised Turkish resistance to the partition of their country had hoped that the armistice would be a prelude to peace with honour. Nevertheless, they had taken the precaution, wherever possible, of moving troops and weapons to the interior of Anatolia out of reach of the Allied armies. When hostilities ended their main concern was to retain command of those troops that were still under arms and to frustrate Allied efforts to disarm them. By and large they retained control of the War Ministry in Istanbul until Damad Ferid, the trusted man of the Sultan and of the Allies, became Grand Vizier in March 1919.

After the Young Turkish revolution of 1908 and particularly after the disastrous defeat of Ottoman armies in the Balkan Wars, the CUP had carried out a thorough purge of the senior command. They also put an end to the inflation of senior ranks to which Sultan Abdülhamid had had recourse to win the army's loyalty. Commanders who survived the CUP purge had their ranks reduced, and promotion during the First World War had to be won on merit and was, in any case, slow. Mustafa Kemal was a colonel when he commanded a key sector in Gallipoli, and a brigadier when he was put in charge of whole armies on the eastern and southern fronts. İsmet (İnönü), who was his chief of staff on the eastern front in 1916, was still a colonel when he was appointed under-secretary at the War Office a week before the armistice. It was this policy which Damad Ferid tried to reverse when he assumed office. Unsuccessful elderly generals purged by the CUP before the outbreak of the war were reinstated. A glaring example was the appointment as Military Governor of İzmir, just prior to the Greek occupation of the city, of the Ottoman commander who had surrendered Salonica to the Greeks in 1912.

The fate of İzmir strengthened the resolve of Turkish nationalist officers to retain control of the War Ministry and through it of appointments in the interior. By the time the Allies realised the key role of the War Ministry in Istanbul and moved to occupy it, Turkish military resistance had taken shape out of their reach. Three young generals, Mustafa Kemal (Atatürk), Kâzım Karabekir and Ali Fuad (Cebesoy) had hoodwinked the Sultan and his Grand Vizier and secured command of forces which became the nucleus of a new Turkish national army. The first to leave Istanbul was Ali Fuad, a close friend and companion of Mustafa Kemal from their days as cadets in the Istanbul War College. He took up command of the army corps in central Anatolia which had its headquarters in Ankara, the eastern railhead of

İSMET (İNÖNÜ)

İsmet (İnönü) (1884–1973), Mustafa Kemal's faithful lieutenant, was a professional soldier. Trained as an artillery officer, he joined the CUP on his first posting to Edirne (Adrianople). In the First World War, he served as Mustafa Kemal's chief of staff on the eastern front and then as corps commander in Palestine. Appointed under-secretary in the War Ministry, he joined Mustafa Kemal in Ankara in 1920 and was made commander of the western front. He beat back the Greeks twice at the Battle of İnönü (after which he was named). After the final Turkish victory against the Greeks, he was the chief Turkish negotiator at the armistice talks in Mudanya, and then at the Lausanne Peace Conference (1922–3), where he put his deafness to good use when he resisted Allied demands. Except for a brief interval in the first years of the republic, he served Atatürk as Prime Minister, until a year before the first president's death in November 1938, when he succeeded him. After organising the Republic's first free elections, he was voted out in 1950, to return as Prime Minister after the military coup of 1960. He lost office in 1965, and retired from politics in 1972. İsmet (İnönü) is remembered as the 'Hero of Lausanne', and the president who kept Turkey out of the Second World War and then oversaw the transition to democratic politics.

a branch line of the incomplete Istanbul-Baghdad railway. Ali Fuad was followed by Kâzım Karabekir who was appointed commander of the army corps in the eastern Anatolian fortress town of Erzurum. This was the largest concentration of Turkish troops after demobilisation. But it numbered only some 18,000 men.[1]

Mustafa Kemal left Istanbul on 16 May, the day after the Greek landing in İzmir. He was armed with wide-ranging powers as inspector of all the Ottoman troops in eastern Turkey with additional jurisdiction covering most of unoccupied Anatolia where he could issue orders both to military commanders and to the civil administration. A few days later, Rauf (Orbay), who had resigned his commission in the navy, left Istanbul for the eastern shores of the Sea of Marmara.

Himself of Caucasian origin, Rauf rallied to the Turkish resistance the warlike Circassians who had been settled on the eastern approaches to the capital in the second half of the 19th century when they were expelled by the Russians from their ancestral lands in the western Caucasus. The commander of the Turkish division stationed in the area was also a Circassian, and was ready to resist foreign occupation.

After his return from the Syrian front in November 1918, Mustafa Kemal had made use of all his political contacts to secure the post of War Minister in the governments which were formed in quick succession after the armistice. In several audiences he tried to reinforce the favourable opinion which the Sultan had formed of him during their trip to Germany in the last year of the War. But although he was known as a critic of the CUP leadership, he had been a member of the CUP, and the perennial losers of the Liberal Union, who came to power when Damad Ferid became Grand Vizier, did not trust him fully. Moreover, Mustafa Kemal was notoriously ambitious and, therefore, a threat to people who had finally achieved office. But suspicious as they were, the Sultan and Damad Ferid needed a commander who had influence with the remnants of the Ottoman army. The superannuated generals they rescued from obscurity were clearly incapable of ensuring the loyalty to the throne of serving officers.

The Allies had threatened to occupy areas where public order was disturbed. There had been some bandit activity in the hinterland of İzmir, although the disturbance this caused was minor in comparison with what would follow the Greek occupation. Greeks lived also in considerable numbers along the shores of the Black Sea, with prosperous Greek communities in most coastal towns, while the interior was dominated by Muslims. Many of these Pontic Greeks (named after the

Euxine Pontus, the name by which the Black Sea was known in classical antiquity), had emigrated to Russia, particularly after the Russian conquest of the Caucasus, and were now in flight from the Bolsheviks. Returning to the Ottoman shores of the Black Sea, they swelled the number of local Greeks who, with their clergy in the lead, were now clamouring for a Christian Pontus state, which would recreate the kingdom of the Comnenes, the last Byzantine dominion to be captured by the Ottoman Turks. Venizelos, with his eyes fixed on Aegean Turkey and ultimately on Constantinople/Istanbul, thought it more practicable to have a Greek-Armenian state around Trebizond/Trabzon, on the assumption that local Armenians deported from the area would return. In either case, local Turks felt threatened. Known as Lazes, although the Laz, properly speaking, lived only in the eastern portion of the Ottoman Black Sea coast, where they preserved their ancestral tongue, akin to Georgian, they were late converts to Islam, and, after the fashion of late converts, passionate in defence of their faith. Living in a narrow strip squeezed between the mountains and the sea, they found an outlet for their energy as seamen, but also as bandits moving in and out of their mountain hideouts.

In April 1919, the Sultan's government sent out 'Commissions of Admonition' led by Ottoman princes to persuade its subjects of different faiths to live peacefully together. It was a vain attempt, as the leaders of Christian communities, Greeks and such Armenians as survived or had returned, were determined to break away from the Ottoman state and refused to have anything to do with the imperial princes. Nor were the Muslims impressed. The princes sent out on safari looked down on the natives. On his arrival in Trabzon, Prince Cemalettin found the boys of the local high school too noisy and complained to the headmaster. 'Your school,' he wrote, 'is as noisy as a synagogue full of Jews chanting their prayers. Is this row a premonition of a rebellion in the country? Or is it that you are not in control of the school? We would like to know.'[2]

The Prince, and his master the Sultan, were soon to find out. But in the meantime, the Sultan and his Grand Vizier understood that it was not enough to send out princes to admonish rebellious subjects. Only the army could re-establish order and, the palace hoped, thus deprive the Allies of an excuse to intervene. Receiving Mustafa Kemal on the eve of his departure for eastern Anatolia, the Sultan said to him: 'Pasha, you have already rendered many services to the state. They are now part of history. Forget about them, for the service you are about to render will be more important still. You can save the state.'[3] Apologists for the Sultan claim that this suggests he had sent out Mustafa Kemal for the express (and secret) purpose of organising resistance to the partition plans of the Allies. The claim is disproved by the Sultan's own proclamation in exile when he accused Mustafa Kemal of breaking his oath of allegiance and of becoming an unbearable source of trouble for the nation.[4]

'Pasha, you have already rendered many services to the state. They are now part of history. Forget about them, for the service you are about to render will be more important still. You can save the state.'
SULTAN VAHDETTIN TO MUSTAFA KEMAL

It was not an accusation which weighed heavily on Mustafa Kemal's conscience. But many of his fellow-commanders found it difficult to break with centuries of Ottoman imperial tradition. The Muslim inhabitants of Anatolia were even less ready to abandon their sovereign. Some, like the Circassians, were pulled both ways. They had experienced foreign oppression in the Caucasus and were determined not to be subjected to it in their new home. But they were passionate in their loyalty to the Sultan-Caliph. There was no Turkish popular revolt against the monarchy as there had been in Russia, Germany and Austria-Hungary. Most Muslims did not blame the Sultan, who had been largely powerless since the rise to power of the Young Turks, but rather the CUP leadership which had involved the country in a catastrophic war. The division between the largely illiterate, conservative Muslim masses and a ruling class schooled in Western culture, which had developed gradually since the introduction of the first reforms in the 19th century, had deepened as a result of the miscalculations of the Young Turks. In the eyes of the mass of Muslims, the Unionists, as the Young Turks were known in the country, were impious bunglers. The fact that resistance to foreign occupation was led by Unionists, however critical these may have been of the CUP leadership, had to be downplayed. Moreover, the Muslim population had been decimated by the war. The survivors were hungry and largely destitute. It was widely believed that the Young Turk leaders, or at least their friends, had enriched themselves while the country suffered.

The accusations were false as far as the CUP leaders were concerned. Outside their ranks as well there were probably fewer war profiteers in Turkey than in other belligerent countries. One reason was that Muslim Turks were new to trade which had been the preserve of foreigners and of native Christians and Jews. In industry, Turks provided only 15 per cent of the capital and of the workforce.[5] The CUP had tried to redress the balance through their 'national', or more accurately nationalist, economic policy. But this was in its early stages. The political power of the Young Turks had not yet translated into wealth. Such little wealth as there was in the countryside was in the hands of individual landowners or, particularly in the Kurdish areas, of tribal leaders, some of whom doubled up as sheikhs – leaders of Muslim fraternities. Sixty-five per cent of the total agricultural area belonged to feudal lords and large landowners,[6] but their holdings yielded little revenue because of lack of investment and an acute shortage of manpower.

Popular resistance to the country's partition was ideological only in the sense that Muslim religious sentiment was important in animating it. However, the main stimulus was fear of dispossession at the hands of Christian minorities, which had been richer than their Muslim neighbours. During and immediately before the war, some 113,000 Turkish families, most of them refugees from the Balkans, had been settled on the Aegean coast, mainly around İzmir, in the property of deported Greeks. When Greek troops occupied the area in 1919, the original owners returned and some 80,000 Turkish settlers fled to the interior.[7] This was exactly what Venizelos wanted. In a memorandum to Lloyd George, the Greek Prime Minister had suggested that intermigration should be encouraged between Greeks who lived outside the area in western Turkey which he claimed and Turks within the area.[8] His aim was not the continued co-existence of Greeks and Turks in a mixed society but the creation of new nationally homogeneous states.

In eastern Anatolia most of the 860,000 Armenians who lived in the area before the war[9] had been deported. The Muslims who took over their property, and who were themselves destitute as a result of the war, resisted restitution. In the parts of southern Anatolia bordering on Syria, which the French occupied at the end of 1918, some of the 150,000 or so Armenians who had been deported began to return and reclaim their property. It was in these areas that popular resistance to Allied occupation arose spontaneously.

Even before nationalist commanders took charge, Muslims began to form societies which campaigned against the extension of foreign rule. The first was the National Defence Society in eastern Thrace founded in December 1918. Paradoxically, there were more Greeks in Turkish eastern Thrace than in western Thrace, an area with a Muslim majority which had passed from the Ottomans to the Bulgarians and then to the Greeks. The chief city of eastern Thrace was Edirne (Adrianople), the second capital of the Ottoman Sultans, who had built some of their most splendid monuments there. All Turks were bound to resist its loss. In the Aegean area, when the first Greek advance stopped at the Milne Line, Turkish resistance took shape outside it and found expression in a congress of anti-annexation societies. In the east, similar societies were formed in Trabzon/Trebizond and in Erzurum, areas coveted by local Greeks and Armenians. They joined forces in the Society for the Defence of Rights of the Eastern Provinces, a title which came to be adopted by civilian nationalist organisations throughout the country.

The title derived from the 'rights of nations' which President Wilson had proclaimed in a speech to the US Congress. But it also had a deeper, revolutionary resonance, echoing the third article of the Declaration of the Rights of Man, voted by the French National Assembly in 1789. This proclaimed that 'the principle of all sovereignty resides essentially in the nation'. The slogan of national rights pointed to the leading role of the Young Turks in these civil self-defence organisations. They were joined by local clerics, usually muftis, who in Ottoman times, as now, were civil servants, and by local Muslim notables, usually landowners. The societies were the civilian base on which nationalist commanders relied to mobilise resistance to the foreigner and provide a semblance of legitimate authority to their efforts to enlist men and requisition supplies.

Even with local support, nationalist commanders needed time to assemble the remnants of the Ottoman army and lay hands on sufficient weapons to take the field. While they were preparing for a renewal of the armed struggle, armed resistance came from a traditional quarter. Throughout most of its history, and particularly when central authority was weak, Anatolia was prey to bandits. After the First World War, bands which had formed around renowned local outlaws were joined by tens of thousands of army deserters seeking refuge in the mountains and in the vast areas of abandoned countryside in the peninsula.

In western Turkey, the outlaws were known as *zeybek*, and their leaders as *efe*. They wore characteristic clothes – bandoliers slung over colourful jerkins and baggy trousers, and they had developed their own forms of folk dance, which passed also to their Christian neighbours and survive in the popular *zeybekiko* music in Greece. Revered today as folk heroes to whom monuments are erected, the *zeybeks* and their *efe* leaders protected and preyed upon the settled population in equal measure. Local Christians and the foreign troops (Greeks in the west, French south of the Taurus mountains) with which Ottoman Christians made common cause, knew them simply as *çete* (usually spelled [*t*]*cheté* in contemporary documents) or bands. Turkish nationalist commanders renamed them 'national (meaning popular) forces' (*kuva-yı milliye*). They tried to control them, stiffening them with regular army officers whenever they could.

Local Turkish administrators, threatened with the loss of their jobs, and landowners, who feared the loss of their land, helped the militias. Landlords were, in any case, used to employing outlaws or raising their own militias in order to hold their own against rivals, bandits and tax collectors. The numbers of militia bands varied, as between raids many of their members returned to their villages where they were indistinguishable from other peasants. The best-known militia or outlaw leader was Demirci (Blacksmith) Mehmet Efe in the hilly country round the valley of the Menderes/Great Meander. There were some 1,800 armed men under his command divided into a dozen or so detachments.[10] Local Christians also had their militias, the best-known among which was the Greek *Mavri Mira* (Black Destiny) band, operating in the area of İzmit (Nicomedia) on the eastern approaches to Istanbul. But as the Greeks had a regular army in the field, the role of their militias was more limited.

The building-blocks of Turkish resistance were thus in place when the War ended. But they could only be assembled when the danger of dispossession at the hands of local Christians and their foreign protectors overcame the weariness of the Turkish population whose first care was to keep body and soul together. This danger became acute first in the east and south as the Armenians began to move in and then in the west when Greek troops landed in İzmir on 15 May 1919. Elsewhere, in central Anatolia round the city of Konya (known as the centre of the Whirling Dervishes and of intense Muslim piety), in the countryside round Ankara, and also in some Kurdish mountain areas, which were not directly threatened, people feared that the nationalists might compromise their precarious survival, which they thought might be secured more effectively if they chose obedience to the Sultan and his Grand Vizier. The nationalists therefore had to mobilise support where they could, persuading reluctant peasants in some places, and suppressing resistance to their plans in others. Nationalist commanders told the Kurds that if they made common cause with the British they would fall prey to the Armenians rather than achieve self-rule. Where persuasion failed, nationalist leaders had recourse to the violence of punitive expeditions and of revolutionary courts. Resistance which lacks the cover of a recognised government has to fight on several fronts and needs both to elicit support and to inspire fear. But before all else, it needs leadership and organisation. This is what Mustafa Kemal provided.

On 19 May 1919 Mustafa Kemal arrived in Samsun, a port lying at the centre of Turkey's Black Sea coast. Informed of his arrival, Kâzım Karabekir invited him to proceed eastwards to his headquarters in Erzurum where the Defence of Rights Societies of Eastern Turkey were about to meet. Instead, Mustafa Kemal travelled inland south to Amasya, a picturesque town situated in a narrow river valley, where a Turkish regiment was quartered. At the height of Ottoman power, Amasya was where imperial princes were sent as governors to learn the art of statecraft. Mustafa Kemal chose it because he could act as host there to a meeting of nationalist leaders. He was joined by Ali Fuad from Ankara and Rauf who had travelled from the shores of the Sea of Marmara. Military commanders were contacted throughout the country and their agreement was obtained to a statement declaring that the Ottoman government in Istanbul was incapable of defending the national interest, and summoning delegates from every Turkish province to make their way to a congress in Sivas in order to take the country's destiny into their hands. In the meantime nationalist commanders and civil governors were not to surrender their posts to the Istanbul government's appointees. It was a first step to the formation of an alternative government in Anatolia, and, although none of the commanders dissented, some had reservations.

Mustafa Kemal had arrived in Anatolia as the Sultan's representative. It did not take long for British control officers in Anatolia to realise that instead of overseeing the disarming of Turkish troops and preventing attacks on local Greeks, Mustafa Kemal had set about organising Turkish national resistance to the Allies. At the insistence of the British High Commissioner, the Sultan's government recalled Mustafa Kemal to Istanbul. But he was now outside their control. From Amasya he travelled east to Erzurum where he arrived still wearing his uniform as an Ottoman brigadier with the cordon of honorary ADC to the Sultan. As the Sultan moved to sack him, Mustafa Kemal resigned his commission. Although he was not himself prepared to break free from Istanbul right away, Kâzım Karabekir stood by Mustafa Kemal and eased the way to his election, first, to the chair of the Erzurum Congress of Eastern Anatolian Defence of Rights Societies, and then to the presidency of its permanent executive (called the Representative Committee), which became the nucleus of an alternative government in Anatolia. The Erzurum Congress adopted the first text of what became known as the National Pact which proclaimed the sovereign independence and indivisibility of Ottoman lands within the armistice lines of November 1918.

Leaving Karabekir in Erzurum, Mustafa Kemal made his way to Sivas where enough provincial delegates had assembled to justify the claim that they represented the whole country.

After a desultory discussion of the possibility of accepting an American Mandate, which the US Congress was in any case unwilling to take on, the Sivas Congress re-affirmed the National Pact, and demanded that the nation should be consulted before the conclusion of a peace treaty, and that the Ottoman government should be represented at the Peace Conference by delegates enjoying the people's trust.

While the nationalist congress was in progress, a British officer, Captain Edward Noel of the Indian Army, made his way from Istanbul to the town of Malatya in south-eastern Turkey where he tried to mobilise the Kurds against Turkish nationalists. Kurdish tribal leaders who aspired to independence had formed in Istanbul a Society for the Advancement of Kurdistan, which sought British support for its ambitions. Captain Noel took up their cause, but his efforts, far from undermining Turkish nationalist resistance, provided Mustafa Kemal with a propaganda weapon. The Kurds were incapable of united action, and when Mustafa Kemal ordered a detachment of Turkish troops to march on Malatya, Captain Noel and his Kurdish contacts fled to Syria. Mustafa Kemal then made maximum use of the episode to discredit Damad Ferid's government. The charge that the Grand Vizier had sought to incite wild Kurdish tribesmen to march on patriotic Turkish Muslims assembled in Sivas caused indignation in the ranks of the Ottoman ruling class. More than a century earlier, the revolutionary fervour of colonists in British North America had been similarly stiffened by the accusation that King George's generals had incited the 'Redskins' against their kith and kin.

Damad Ferid had resigned in the aftermath of the Greek occupation of İzmir. The Sultan immediately asked him to form a new cabinet into which respected elder statesmen

– the former Grand Viziers Ahmet İzzet and Tevfik – were co-opted. The imperial decree re-appointing the Grand Vizier declared in ringing tones: 'At this crucial moment, when all members of the nation led by their Caliph and Sultan, the head of the six-and-a half-centuries-old dynasty, sprung from the nation's bosom, who is himself ready for any sacrifice, are united in the single aspiration to safeguard the nation in its entirety, we demand that you should devote all your energy to this sacred national cause.'[11] The Sultan was indeed ready for any sacrifice except that of his throne.

Originally the Allies had not intended to invite Ottoman representatives to the Peace Conference before they had agreed the terms of the settlement among themselves. But the French did not want Damad Ferid to look exclusively to the British for protection. They promised that he would be heard in Paris and arranged transport for him and his delegation on board a French warship. On 17 June, a month after the landing of Greek troops in İzmir, Damad Ferid presented a memorandum to the Allies in which he blamed the CUP leadership for Turkey's entry into the war, and likened the Unionists to the Bolsheviks. 'Now,' he said, 'just as the Allies are trying to liberate the Slav people, so too they should extend their help to the Turkish people in kindness and humanity.' He then outlined his proposals, which he filled out in a second memorandum on 23 June. Even as a first bargaining position, Damad Ferid's proposals were pitched high. Not only did he ask for the territorial integrity of the Ottoman Empire to be respected, but he claimed also the Greek islands close to the Turkish coast and western Thrace which had been lost in the Balkan Wars. The Arabs could have self-rule under princes appointed by the Sultan who would also remain patron of the Muslim shrines in Arabia.

The Allies rubbed their eyes in astonishment and delivered a stinging riposte. The Turks, they said, had proved themselves incapable of ruling other races. Wherever they went, they caused destruction and the loss of prosperity and cultural vitality, which recovered only after their departure. The Allies respected Islam, but the Turks would do better in 'appropriate conditions' – in other words, cut down to size. The reply was as absurd in its insulting generalisations and national stereotypes as Damad Ferid had been in his expectations. The Allies then told Damad Ferid that they had other pressing business to attend to, and that his continued presence in Paris would serve no useful purpose. He would be informed in due course when the Allies had decided among themselves the terms of the Turkish peace settlement.[12] Damad Ferid returned to Istanbul empty-handed and discredited, just as Mustafa Kemal was rallying the forces of Turkish nationalism and Muslim resistance in Anatolia.

As the Allies were still busy with the European peace settlement, and with Greek occupation troops corralled behind the Milne Line, the Sultan gave way to Turkish nationalist pressure. Damad Ferid resigned on 2 October 1919, barely three weeks after the conclusion of the nationalist congress in Sivas, and was replaced by Ali Rıza Pasha, a 60-year-old Field Marshal who had been the unsuccessful commander of the Ottoman Western Army in the Balkan War. In line with the demands of the nationalists, the Sultan decreed that parliamentary elections should be held before a peace settlement was negotiated. The new Grand Vizier made an effort to reaffirm Ottoman sovereignty in the capital, demanding that local Greeks who were Ottoman subjects should not fly the Greek flag. He tried to heal the breach with Mustafa Kemal and despatched his Navy Minister, Salih Hulusi (another superannuated general) to negotiate with him. Nothing came of the attempt. Local Greeks refused to have anything to do with the elections, held in December 1919, which were won handsomely by Turkish nationalists.

Mustafa Kemal had in the meantime left Sivas for Ankara, which had direct railway communications with Istanbul. He stood for election, but refused to go to Istanbul when elected to the new parliament. However, most of his companions, who were also successful in the elections, travelled to Istanbul, in spite of Mustafa Kemal's insistence that the new parliament should meet in unoccupied Anatolia, just as the German parliament had met not in Berlin, but in Weimar. Left alone in Anatolia, Mustafa Kemal's control over his sympathisers in the new parliament became tenuous. Although some disagreements surfaced, parliament reaffirmed the National Pact, stiffening it with the demand that popular referendums should also be held in western Thrace and in the three provinces which the Ottomans had regained from Tsarist Russia to determine whether local people wanted to be part of an independent Ottoman state. On 17 February 1920, parliament voted to communicate the National Pact to all Allied parliaments.

The nationalist stand of the Ottoman parliament under the complacent eyes of the Ali Rıza government was too much for the British occupation authorities, which were not mollified when Ali Rıza resigned and was replaced by Salih Hulusi Pasha, the go-between chosen to bring Mustafa Kemal back into the Ottoman fold. On 16 March 1920, with the reluctant assent of the other Allies, British troops occupied the Ottoman War Ministry and the barracks of Ottoman troops in the capital. There was some firing and a few Turkish soldiers were killed. A Turkish telegraph clerk, a refugee from

Macedonia called Hamdi, achieved national fame by keeping open the line to Ankara and informing Mustafa Kemal's headquarters of the progress of the British occupation. He then made his way to Ankara and, many years later, when it was decreed that all Turks should have surnames, he chose the surname 'Sixteenth March'.

British troops moved to arrest the leading nationalists in the newly-elected parliament, which immediately adjourned without fixing a date for a new session. Rauf, who had returned to Istanbul as a member of parliament, was among the exiles sent to Malta. The forcible entry into a freely elected Ottoman parliament of the troops of a country which prided itself on being the mother of parliaments provided Turkish nationalists with useful propaganda ammunition. There were to be no further sessions of the Ottoman parliament. The Sultan dissolved it, and his government could not organise new elections, as its authority did not extend much beyond the capital. Salih Hulusi resigned and was replaced yet again by Damad Ferid, a man utterly incapable of rallying the country round him.

In the confusion caused by the British occupation and the change of government, those Turkish nationalists who had not been rounded up made their way to Ankara. They included not only members of parliament, but also military commanders, notably General Fevzi Çakmak, the most senior Ottoman officer to side with Mustafa Kemal, and Colonel İsmet (İnönü), Mustafa Kemal's faithful, but careful lieutenant, who always looked before he leapt. Fevzi had earlier tried to turn Kâzım Karabekir against Mustafa Kemal, but this was not held against him. Mustafa Kemal shared the esteem in which Fevzi was held in the Turkish officer corps, and made him Chief of Staff of the new Turkish national army.

The Allied occupation of Istanbul sealed Mustafa Kemal's leadership of the Turkish nationalist movement and allowed him to take the next step. This was to summon a national assembly in Ankara as a prelude to the formation of a fully-fledged alternative government. The assembly called itself the Grand National Assembly and its executive became known as the Government of the Grand National Assembly. The adjective 'Turkish' was to be added later: at first the fiction was maintained that it was the Ottoman nation which was represented.

Mustafa Kemal saw to it that his parliament and government appealed to all and sundry Muslims and Turks. The Assembly was made up of those deputies of the last Ottoman parliament who managed to make their way to Istanbul and of new members elected *ad hoc*, or, more accurately co-opted by nationalists in Societies for the Defence of Rights or by provincial notables. Some of the members of the new assembly were deemed to represent occupied areas where no elections could be held. All the members were united in their determination to resist foreign rule. But they were not of one mind when it came to tactics, and were ready to criticise the nationalist leadership when things went wrong, and to limit as far as possible the power of Mustafa Kemal, who was suspected of nurturing dictatorial ambitions.

The Assembly held its first meeting on 23 April 1920 under the slogan 'sovereignty belongs unconditionally to the nation'. This revolutionary sentiment was reflected also in the powers which the Assembly arrogated to itself, combining the functions of the legislature, executive and judiciary. Elected president of the Assembly, Mustafa Kemal was also head of government, which took the title of Committee of Executive Commissioners. The commissioners were elected singly by the Assembly which could also dismiss them. The inspiration came from the French National Convention after the 1789 Revolution, but also from the Bolshevik Committee of Executive Commissars (known by the Russian abbreviation *ispolkom*). From the start, Mustafa Kemal (and to a lesser extent Kâzım Karabekir in Erzurum) tried to secure the support of the Bolsheviks, while keeping them out of the country. Ideologies were fluid, misconceptions flourished, and contradictory views were held, genuinely or for tactical reasons.

The opening of the revolutionary Assembly was marked with an Islamic ritual, excessive even by late Ottoman standards. It took place on a Friday when all male adult Muslims are meant to pray as a congregation. After prayers in the main Ankara mosque (which was also a shrine to a local holy man), members of the Assembly walked in procession preceded by a cleric holding a relic – one of the many supposed hairs from the beard of the Prophet Muhammad, venerated in the country. Imams throughout unoccupied Anatolia were ordered to recite not only the whole of the Koran, but also a lengthy compendium of the sayings attributed to the Prophet. Sheep were sacrificed in Ankara and the provinces to invoke divine blessing.

After these preliminaries, the Assembly met in the building which had served as the premises of the club of the Young Turks. It was built in what became known in Turkey as the 'national style', although Western colonial architecture from French North Africa to the British Federated Malay States, was a more obvious source of inspiration. Refurbished and enlarged, the building was later used by the Turkish parliament for many years, then by the Republican People's Party, which Mustafa Kemal founded, and is now preserved as a museum.

The first act of the revolutionary Assembly was to send a message of loyalty to the Sultan, who was deemed to have become the captive of the Allies and to be surrounded by evil ministers who kept him ignorant of his subjects' concerns. But while the fiction was maintained, Mustafa Kemal made sure that even those members of the Ottoman dynasty who were sympathetic to the nationalist cause were kept out of Anatolia. In April 1921, Prince Ömer Faruk, son of the heir apparent Abdülmecid, eluded Allied controls and travelled secretly to the small port of İnebolu on the Black Sea which the nationalists controlled and which served as the point of entry to unoccupied Anatolia. At Mustafa Kemal's instructions, he was sent back to Istanbul and told that the time to make use of his services would come later.

Mustafa Kemal was a master tactician who used fictions when they served his purpose. He sought support wherever he could find it. In order to get help both from the Bolsheviks and from foreign Muslims, he went along with the argument that the Muslim world and Bolshevism had a common enemy in imperialism, and that they were, at least to some extent, compatible. Misconceptions reinforced useful fiction. Addressing a Bolshevik envoy, Mustafa Kemal declared *Turkey is engaged in a determined and vital endeavour, because it is battling in the cause of all oppressed nations, of the whole Orient.*

'Turkey is engaged in a determined and vital endeavour, because it is battling in the cause of all oppressed nations, of the whole Orient.'
MUSTAFA KEMAL

There was at the time of the Russian Civil War a ragged armed band, led by the anti-Semitic peasant bandit Makhno, which styled itself the Green Army. As green is the colour of Islam, some supporters of Turkish national resistance believed that the Green Army had been formed by Muslim Communists, and they set up a similar organisation in unoccupied Anatolia. Also called the Green Army, it attracted the Circassians who resisted control even by their fellow-Muslims. But in addition to undisciplined rebel fighters, there was also a small group of Marxists in Turkey, usually rebellious children of the ruling class who had been impressed by the Spartacist movement in Germany and had pinned their hopes on the world-wide revolution preached by the Bolsheviks.

While Mustafa Kemal was consolidating his power in Ankara, the Allies continued to dither. But a peace settlement with Turkey could not be put off forever. The Versailles Treaty with Germany was signed on 28 June 1919. The treaty with Austria followed. It was signed at St Germain, also near Paris, on 10 September. Third came the treaty with Bulgaria, signed at Neuilly, in the same vicinity, on 27 November. There was a delay before the treaty with Hungary was signed at Trianon on 4 June 1920. (There was no shortage of royal palaces near Paris.) All these treaties left a legacy of bitterness which erupted in the Second World War, when the nationalist leaders of defeated nations made common cause with Nazi Germany. The Turkish settlement was more difficult, but when it finally came it proved more durable. The rise of modern Turkey provides a perfect illustration of the law of unintended consequences – in this case the beneficial consequences of Lloyd George's ill-advised policy. But an immense price in human suffering had to be paid before the benefits finally emerged.

The government which Damad Ferid formed on 5 May 1919 after the British had raided the Ottoman parliament did all it could to strangle at birth the nationalist movement in Anatolia. A week into its tenure of power, it procured from the Sheikh al-Islam, the head of the official clerical establishment in Istanbul, a fatwa declaring that the nationalist forces were rebels against the faith and that it was the duty of all Muslims to kill them. The nationalists responded by obtaining a counter-fatwa from the muftis of Anatolia, with the mufti of Ankara in the lead, saying that, on the contrary, it was the duty of all good Muslims to resist foreign occupation and free the Sultan-Caliph from foreign captivity. (Throughout Ottoman history fatwas were issued with the ease of vending machines: you put in a coin and got your fatwa.) The National Assembly in Ankara passed a law declaring that people who resisted its authority would be guilty of high treason. In Istanbul a court-martial passed death sentences on Mustafa Kemal and his companions.

The war of words was reflected by clashes on the ground, as rebellions broke out in nationalist-held territory. Damad Ferid's government formed a 'disciplinary force', known also as the Army of the Caliphate, to suppress the nationalists. The pay it offered attracted a ragbag of none-too-enthusiastic volunteers, whom the nationalists had little difficulty in putting to flight. The rebellions behind the lines held by the nationalists posed a greater problem, but these too were suppressed, often by militias. Circassians who supported the nationalists routed their fellow-tribesmen loyal to the Sultan. Similarly, Kurdish tribes fought each other, and those which sided with the nationalists helped the weak national army to establish the authority of the National Assembly. Nevertheless Mustafa Kemal felt personally threatened when the feudal clan which dominated the district of Yozgat, just east of Ankara, rebelled against his authority. The army was unable to suppress the rising, and the nationalists' Circassian allies had to be rushed from their territory west of Ankara to do the job. Their leader, Edhem, commander of the 'mobile force' of horsemen, and patron of the Green Army, got ideas above his station and strutted around like a bully when he showed up in Ankara with his fighters. He got his come-uppance a few months later when the new regular national army took over the command of militias. Refusing to submit to the discipline of the new nationalist regime, Edhem and the remnant of his forces sought refuge with the Greeks. He ended up in Transjordan, where fellow-Circassians provided the guard of Abdullah, whom the British had installed as emir.

On the ground, the military situation remained frozen for a year after the Greek occupation of İzmir and the surrounding area in May 1919. But while the wheels of diplomacy slowly ground forward, the Allies demobilised in response to domestic discontent. When the Paris Peace Conference opened, Lloyd George made much of the fact that there were more than one million British troops occupying Ottoman territory.[13] A few months later their numbers fell to little over 300,000, and these were fully occupied holding Mesopotamia and Palestine, with only a weak force guarding the Turkish Straits and occupying Istanbul. This led to the next step in the destruction of Anatolia.

In the night of 14/15 June 1920 Turkish nationalist detachments outside İzmit clashed with a weak British force guarding the town which controlled access to Istanbul from the east. The British commander, General George Milne, asked London for reinforcements. None were available, and the Chief of the Imperial General Staff proposed that a Greek division should be used to defend the Ottoman capital. Venizelos was only too ready to oblige with a division stationed in western Thrace. His reward was the permission for Greek troops to occupy eastern Thrace, including Edirne, and to cross the Milne Line to seize the whole of western Anatolia, south of the Sea of Marmara.[14]

The first steps leading to the disastrous decision to impose draconian peace terms on Turkey were taken at Allied consultations in London between 12 February and 10 March 1920. At a meeting on 16 February, Venizelos pressed his claims to İzmir and the surrounding area on the basis of population statistics, which exaggerated the number of Greeks and undercounted the Turks. He was supported by Lloyd George. The London conference was followed by the extension of British military control in Istanbul on 16 March, but not before the British High Commissioner in the Ottoman capital had outlined his fears. 'The terms are such that no Turks … can very well accept,' wrote Admiral de Robeck. He warned that the Allies would have to be prepared 'for a resumption of general warfare'. Moreover, they would 'do violence to their own declared and cherished principles … and perpetuate bloodshed indefinitely in the Near East'.[15]

The French had similar reservations. On 12 February 1920, the day that the London conference opened, their troops had been forced by a local uprising to evacuate Maraş in southern Turkey. The uprising was led by an imam, known as 'the Milkman'. The memory of this episode has been kept alive. Today, the town is known officially as Kahramanmaraş (Maraş the Heroic), and it boasts of the University of the Milkman Imam. Some of the Armenians who had accompanied the French troops were killed during the evacuation, giving rise to reports of an Armenian massacre. Having experienced Turkish resistance, the new French Prime Minister Alexandre Millerand persuaded the Allies to commission a report from the military commission chaired in Versailles by Marshal Ferdinand Foch, the victorious commander on the

Western Front. Foch concluded that no less than 27 divisions would be required to impose the terms demanded by Lloyd George and his protégé Venizelos.[16] Although he was warned by Lloyd George that he could expect no help, Venizelos promised rashly that his army could do it alone. The Italians, who had been cheated out of their main prize, expressed their doubts. Nevertheless, the final plan to partition Turkey was agreed at a conference of Allied leaders at San Remo between 19 and 26 of April, just as Mustafa Kemal's nationalist government was taking shape in Ankara. There was only one way of enforcing the Allied peace terms. On 21 June at a meeting in Boulogne, the Allied leaders allowed the Greek army to occupy eastern Thrace and the whole of western Anatolia.

An Ottoman delegation was summoned to Paris to sign the peace treaty. It was led by the elderly Tevfik Pasha, the Sultan's man for all seasons. On 25 June, the Ottoman delegation submitted its reply to the partition project on which the Allies had agreed at San Remo. Tevfik Pasha had already advised his government that the Allied peace terms were incompatible with the continued existence of an independent Ottoman state. This was strongly argued in the Ottoman reply, which made the point that the Allied peace settlement imposed on the Ottoman government obligations while depriving it of the means to carry them out. The desire to tie down the Turks had been pushed to absurd lengths. Under the Allied plan, there would be eight separate jurisdictions in Istanbul: the Sultan's government, the proposed Straits Commission (with its own flag), the military authorities of the Allied occupation forces, the political authority of the High Commissioners of Britain, France and Italy, the Allied commission for supervision and organisation, the international financial commission, the board of the foreign-owned Ottoman public debt and foreign consular courts applying their own laws. But the Allies were in no mood to listen to reason. Rather than wait for their response, which he could guess in advance, Tevfik turned to the Grand Vizier Damad Ferid, who had joined the delegation, much to the displeasure of the other members, and said: 'There is no point in staying on for there is nothing more we can do. Let us at least save money by returning home and leaving our junior colleagues here.'[17]

On 11 July the Allied leaders met in Spa in Belgium, where the Kaiser had his headquarters during the First World War. Millerand, Curzon, the Italian representative Count Sforza, Viscount Chinda of Japan and Venizelos were there. Sforza was an ironic observer; the Japanese were not really interested; Curzon stuck to Lloyd George's line, in spite of his reservations; and Venizelos made sure that a crushing reply was sent to the Ottoman government. He succeeded. Whatever they might think in private, the Principal Allies agreed on a text that was both uncompromising and insulting.

The Ottoman decision to enter the war on the side of Germany, they declared, was an act of treachery. It prolonged the war by two years and caused the Allies the loss of millions of men and billions in money. After 1914, the reply thundered, the Ottomans had murdered 800,000 Armenians, and deported another 100,000 as well as 200,000 Greeks. The Allies had to guard against further treachery in deciding the regime of the Straits. The accusations led to a final threat: if the Ottoman government did not sign the treaty, or if it was unable to impose its authority in Anatolia, the Allies reserved the right to review their terms and drive the Turks out of Europe for ever. The Ottoman government was given ten days until 27 July to reply to this ultimatum.[18] Prejudice against Turks could go no further. In Britain today this forgotten text would fall foul of the Race Relations Act. But in Turkey it is remembered as the expression of abiding anti-Turkish prejudice, and it has left a mark on attitudes to the outside world.

By the time the Allied ultimatum was received in Istanbul, the whole of coastal Anatolia, with the exception of the shores of the Black Sea, was under foreign occupation. Turkish troops on the ground were too weak to prevent the advance of the Greek army. Isolated in eastern Thrace they had no option but to surrender. In Anatolia, the Greeks swept north and west out of their enclave round İzmir. On 8 July 1920, they occupied Bursa, the second capital of the Ottomans, at the centre of the rich Bithynian plain south of the Sea of Marmara. This was a bitter blow to the Turks, for whom Bursa, like Edirne, symbolised the glories of the Ottoman Empire. As a sign of mourning, the rostrum of the National Assembly in Ankara was draped in black.

Arnold Toynbee, who had earlier worked for the government and helped compile the British *Blue Book* designed to rally the American public to the Allied cause, with stories of Armenian atrocities, took time away from his duties as Professor of Mediaeval and Modern Greek in King's College London in order to report for the *Manchester Guardian*, then as now the voice of British liberalism, on the progress of the Greek occupation of Anatolia. From the eastern approaches of Istanbul, he could see the flames of Turkish villages torched by the Greeks on the eastern shores of the gulf of İzmit. The experience changed his outlook. In *The Western Question in Greece and Turkey*, the book he published in 1922, he came to the conclusion that Greece was 'as incapable as Turkey (or for that matter any Western country) of governing well a mixed population containing an alien majority and a minority of her own nationality'.[19] The Greek shipowners who had funded the chair at King's College were furious. Toynbee was forced to leave. He devoted himself to the development of the Royal Institute of International Affairs and to writing his ten-volume *Study of History*, in which his pessimistic view of Western civilisation found expression in the theory that all civilisations arise as a challenge to a response and that they are all destined to die. Historical, and generally cultural, relativism was a response to Allied triumphalism at the end of the First World War. Eventually, Toynbee gained the admiration of Turks who, unlike him, had no doubts about the values of Western civilisation, whatever the misdeeds committed in its name.

The Allied threat to drive the Turks out of Europe forever cut no ice with the Turkish nationalists who had, in any case, left European Turkey to carry on the fight in Anatolia. But the Sultan was determined not to compromise the prospect of staying on in Istanbul, as a shadowy sovereign claiming to be Caliph of all Muslims. Even so, he decided to summon a council of the throne before agreeing to the Allied demands. His Grand Vizier, Damad Ferid, argued that to reject the terms would be equivalent to committing the sin of suicide. The Ottoman dynasty was like an ancient tree. So long as its roots remained in its native soil, it was capable of new growth. Summoned to choose between a shadowy survival and extinction, the grandees summoned to the council voted in favour of accepting the peace settlement in spite of its 'terrible conditions', There was only one dissenting vote. It was cast by Rıza Pasha, a retired artillery general.

Armed with the authority of the throne council, an Ottoman delegation went to Paris to sign the peace treaty imposed by the Allies. Two of its members – a diplomat and a senator – were inconspicuous. But the third had a considerable, although controversial, reputation. He was the poet, Rıza Tevfik, known as 'the philosopher', philosophy being the subject he taught at the university of Istanbul. He had been a member of the CUP before joining Damad Ferid in the Liberal Union. A liberal and a patriot after his fashion, who believed in the doomed ideal of 'the union of all elements' (the peaceful co-existence of the constituent communities of the Ottoman state), he was listed among the 150 opponents of the nationalists who were exiled after 1923. Together with the surviving exiles, he was pardoned in 1938 and returned to Turkey where he is remembered as an eccentric idealist out of tune with the times.

On 10 August 1920, the Ottoman delegation signed the peace treaty at Sèvres, outside Paris. Critics were not slow to observe that the treaty was as brittle as the porcelain made there for the French court. But it was certainly nothing like as beautiful. On the same day, Britain, France and Italy signed a pact on their respective zones of influence in what remained of Turkey. The Italians were to enjoy preferential treatment in south-western Anatolia, the French in the south and the British in the extreme south-east, north of Iraq. The pact was a British sop to the French, who had given up Mosul, promised to them in the Sykes-Picot agreement, and particularly to the Italians, who lost İzmir and who did not add to their territorial gains – the Dodecanese and Libya – acquired on the eve of the War. But the Italians were not satisfied, and became the first Allies to befriend the Turkish nationalists. The French preferred to wait on events before making their own arrangements. Thus, right from the beginning, two of the Principal Allies did not share Lloyd George's enthusiasm for the Sèvres Treaty. Even Curzon, who had become Foreign Secretary in October 1919, had misgivings. He asked Lloyd

George to 'think seriously' about Anatolia and the Greeks. He was, he said, 'the last man to wish to do a good turn to the Turks', but he wanted to achieve 'something like peace in Asia Minor, which was impossible so long as the Greeks were marching about inside it'.[20]

The Sèvres treaty died 'intact, though dead, whole though unratified' in the words of Andrew Ryan, the Dragoman at the British embassy in Istanbul.[21] Greece was, in fact, the only signatory to ratify it. Six months after the signature of the treaty, a conference had to be arranged in London to amend its more outrageous provisions. But this proved impossible.

Under the Treaty of Sèvres, the Ottoman state was to lose eastern Thrace to Greece, the territory of which would extend right up to the suburbs of Istanbul. Istanbul would remain nominally under Ottoman sovereignty, but as the Ottoman delegates had already pointed out, this would be diluted to vanishing-point. The area around İzmir, known to Greek nationalists and Western Philhellenes by the classical name of Ionia, would also remain under nominal Ottoman sovereignty, but only for five years, after which its fate would be decided by a referendum. The deportation and flight of Turks which followed the Greek occupation had made certain in advance that the referendum would result in the annexation of Ionia to Greece. In the south, French-Mandated Syria would gain a large slice of adjacent Turkish territory. In the east, the Kurds would gain autonomy immediately and independence if they opted for it a year later and the Council of the League of Nations thought they had the capacity for it. Further north, there would be a greater independent Armenia with access to the sea, within borders which were to be decided by President Woodrow Wilson. Wilson announced his award on 22 November 1920, in the dying days of his administration after Congress had refused to ratify the covenant of the League of Nations. The outgoing president generously gave the Armenians the port city of Trabzon, the fortress town of Erzurum, and all the country round Lake Van. Wilson's letter announcing his decision was touching in its optimism. 'It is my confident expectation,' he wrote that 'the Armenian refugees and their leaders ... will by refraining from any and all form of reprisals give the world an example of that high moral courage which must always be the foundation of national strength ... surpassing in the liberality of their administrative arrangements ... even the ample provisions for non-Armenian racial and religious groups embodied in the Minorities Treaty.'[22]

Woodrow Wilson's faith was misplaced. When the newly-established Armenian republic took over the frontier provinces of Russian Transcaucasia from the British, which Turkish troops had evacuated after the armistice, Muslim villages were torched and many of their inhabitants killed. In September 1920, a month after the signature of the Sèvres Treaty, the nationalist government in Ankara authorised Karabekir to cross the old Tsarist frontier. On 30 October he captured the fortress of Kars. This time Armenian civilians fled or were killed. It was the fourth wave of human wretchedness washing over the eastern Anatolian plateau since 1914: Muslim Turks and Kurds escaping the advancing Russians in 1915, while Armenians were being deported and killed in the Turkish rear; Turks fleeing from Armenians who took over from the Russians in February 1917; Armenians escaping from advancing Turks later the same year; and, finally, the two rounds of ethnic cleansing in 1919–20, with Muslims suffering first and Armenians second. No Armenians were left thereafter on the Turkish side of the frontier except for

THE MINORITIES

Non-Muslim communities in the Ottoman Empire enjoyed a large degree of self-government under traditional Muslim canon law. That status had to be adjusted when the equality of all Ottoman subjects was recognised in the 19th century. The reforms did not satisfy nationalists within the non-Muslim communities who sought the support of Christian great powers in their quest for independent statehood. The problem became acute when areas where non-Muslims were concentrated broke away from Ottoman rule, leaving behind scattered non-Muslim communities, which, in the eyes of the Turks, served as an excuse for foreign intervention. Similar problems arose in the successor states of the Austro-Hungarian and Russian empires. The peace treaties negotiated in 1919–20 guaranteed the rights of national and religious minorities which were placed under the protection of the League of Nations. The Polish Minorities Treaty, known as 'the Little Versailles', signed on 28 June 1919, served as a model for bilateral treaties concluded with other states. The unratified Treaty of Sèvres, imposed on the Ottoman Empire, went beyond the Polish Minorities Treaty in granting privileges to non-Muslims who were to remain under Ottoman rule. The Treaty of Lausanne dealt more briefly with the issue, guaranteeing the rights of non-Muslim communities and specifying that similar rights should be enjoyed by Muslims living in Greece. National legislation could not impinge on these rights which were to be protected by the League of Nations. Turkish nationalists argue to this day that minority rights in their country apply only to non-Muslims, while liberals quote Article 39, paragraphs 2–4, which, taken literally, apply to all citizens, irrespective of religion, and provide for the unrestricted use of their mother tongues. Cultural rights figure prominently in the demands of Turkish citizens of Kurdish origin.

those who sought refuge with their Muslim neighbours and converted to Islam. On the Russian side, ethnic cleansing stopped and was replaced by the cleansing of class enemies with the advent of the Bolsheviks, and then resumed and was completed after the dissolution of the Soviet Union some 70 years later.

As its army collapsed, the Armenian government sued for an armistice. On 2 December 1920 the government of the Grand National Assembly signed a peace treaty with Armenia, and Turkey regained the three frontier provinces which it had lost to the Russians in 1878. Soon afterwards the Bolsheviks took over in what remained of Armenia, which was thereafter ruled from Moscow as the Armenian Soviet Socialist Republic. Its coat of arms showed Mount Ararat (Ağrı Dağ in Turkish), but the mountain now lay in Turkish territory. It did not take long for Wilson's award to be mocked by history. Armenian nationalists are still hoping that somehow or other they will regain what Wilson had given them. But if there is, in their eyes, an unredeemed Armenia, there are no unredeemed Armenians, and they are finding it difficult enough as it is to repopulate the territory which they seized from Azerbaijan and ethnically cleansed in the 1980s.

Neither Sultan Vahdettin nor his hated Grand Vizier Damad Ferid signed the Treaty of Sèvres. Forgetting conveniently that he had done his best to stifle opposition to the treaty, the Sultan claimed later that his only motive was to gain time until the balance of external forces moved in Turkey's favour. In Ankara, the Grand National Assembly, under Mustafa Kemal's determined leadership, did not prevaricate. On 19 August, nine days after the signature of the treaty, it declared that the Ottoman signatories and all those in the throne council who had voted in favour of signing were guilty of high treason.

Ineffective as it was, the Sèvres Treaty left a legacy of bitterness which persists to this day. Its authors looked down on the Turks as a people incapable of progress who had to be civilised by external force. They had to make sure that the brakes on their railway carriages were in order (Article 358), that only qualified archaeologists were allowed to dig for antiquities (Article 421, add.7), that the white slave trade was effectively banned (Article 273/6), that obscene publications were banned (Article 273/7) and that birds useful to agriculture were protected (Article 273/11).[23] If to this day it is a criminal offence in Turkey to denigrate 'Turkishness', the reason should be sought in the memory left by the Treaty of Sèvres.

Mustafa Kemal (1881–1938) (*right*) with his Chief of Staff İsmet (İnönü) (1884–1973).

II

Lausanne

4

Western Revolution in the East

It took three years – between August 1920 and July 1923 – for the Principal Allies in the West to lose their original peace settlement and win back Turkey. This happy outcome came about because they did not persist in their errors. Saddled with the enormous cost of victory in the First World War, they did not want to incur further costs as they made such gains as they could in the Near East. When Mustafa Kemal demonstrated that both he and they could emerge with profit from the ruins of the Ottoman Empire, they struck a bargain. But before diplomacy could repair the damage done at Sèvres, a war had to be fought to determine the balance of forces on the ground. The Principal Allies fought it by proxy. The cost was borne by the Turks, Greeks and Armenians who had lived side by side for centuries on the soil of what was to become the Republic of Turkey.

True, the various ethnic communities were complicit in the policies which caused them great suffering. It would be wrong to say that Turks suffered solely because they had been duped by the Germans into the First World War and then by President Wilson's Fourteen Points, or that Greeks and Armenians were the blind victims of the designs of the Principal Allies. The Turks had allowed the CUP to lead them to the brink of destruction, and the Greeks and Armenians similarly allowed their leaders to pursue calamitous policies. If the Great Powers are to be blamed, it is for their failure to shield the ethnic communities from the folly of their leaders, and in some cases for inspiring false hopes.

The Treaty of Sèvres was buried on the battlefields of western Turkey. The casualties suffered by the new regular Turkish army in these battles were comparatively light – 13,000 men killed and 35,000 wounded.[1] The combined losses of the Greek and Armenian armies were much heavier – more than twice as many. But it was the civilian population which suffered most, with hundreds of thousands dying and some three million uprooted. It took a generation before these losses were made good, and when they were, another mistaken assumption which underlay the rickety edifice designed at Sèvres was made manifest. The Greek territorial claims put forward by Venizelos and the Armenian claims accepted by President Wilson were both based on demographic projections which assumed that the Greek and Armenian population would increase fast enough to fill the territories wrenched from Turkey, and faster in any case than the Turkish population. This was the case when Greeks and Armenians were more prosperous and, therefore, healthier than their Turkish neighbours. But peace and medical services reversed the trend. Today the population of Turkey is five times larger than that of Greece and Armenia combined, and there are not enough Greeks and Armenians to realise the dreams of such unreconstructed nationalists as survive in their midst.

Diplomacy and armed resistance went hand in hand under Mustafa Kemal's guidance. The immediate task after

Sèvres was to suppress the risings in the Turkish nationalist rear fomented by the Sultan's government in Istanbul. This was done between August and December 1920. Faced with the failure of his attempts to liquidate the nationalist movement in Anatolia, Damad Ferid resigned on 17 October, and left the country for a rest cure in the spa of Karlsbad (now Karlovy Vary in the Czech Republic). He was to return to Istanbul once only, very briefly in September 1922 when he collected his wife Mediha (the Sultan's sister), other members of the family and such belongings as he could carry away, and slipped off to permanent exile in France. Sultan Vahdettin, who was himself about to follow him, was informed in an impersonal note which read: 'At her husband's insistence, the Princess Mediha left for Europe for treatment two hours ago, as her rheumatism was getting worse here.' Put out, the Sultan remarked pathetically 'The naughty boy! He got the State into this mess and then walked away.'[2] Vahdettin was, of course, himself responsible for bringing the naughty boy to power over and over again. When he had appointed Damad Ferid for the last time after the signature of the Treaty of Sèvres, he was warned by the former Deputy Speaker of Parliament that the appointment would be calamitous for the country and the dynasty. Vahdettin was not dissuaded. 'If I so desired,' he said, 'I could name as Grand Vizier the Greek or Armenian Patriarch or even the Chief Rabbi.' 'You could, Sir,' the Deputy Speaker replied, 'but it wouldn't do you any good.'[3] After Damad Ferid's precipitate final departure, his name never again passed the lips of his exiled sovereign.

Damad Ferid was succeeded once again by the veteran statesman Tevfik Pasha, who was to be the last Grand Vizier of the Ottoman Empire. Tevfik's son was married to the Sultan's daughter, and he was, therefore, trusted as a relative.

Nevertheless, in the proclamation which he issued from exile in Mecca in order to exculpate himself, Vahdeddin claimed that his actions had always been guided by public opinion or by other 'considerations which could not be resisted', and went on: 'The best proof is that I kept Tevfik Pasha in power for more than two years, solely because public opinion was not opposed to him, even although he allowed Kemalists, whose bad intentions towards my person and my position were manifest, to establish their influence in Istanbul.'[4]

In July 1920, a month before the signature of the Sèvres Treaty, Mustafa Kemal had despatched to Moscow his Foreign Minister Bekir Sami (a Turkish nationalist of Caucasian stock). But, just like their Western foes, the Bolsheviks were loath to put their money on Mustafa Kemal before they could see his form. At first they offered unacceptable odds, demanding a slice of eastern Turkey for the Armenians as the price of their support. In any case, there were other Turkish competitors for Moscow gold.

The CUP war leader Enver, who had sought refuge in Germany at the end of the war, managed to get to Moscow with the help of his German friends and canvassed Bolshevik support for a plan to mobilise Muslims worldwide against the British. He was opposed by Turkish Communists subservient to Moscow. Their leader was a Paris-trained radical journalist, Mustafa Suphi. An opponent of the German alliance, he had sought refuge in Russia where he was detained as an enemy alien. Set free after the Bolshevik revolution, he recruited Turkish prisoners of war in Russian camps to help the Red Army, and formed the Turkish Communist Party which was admitted to the Communist International. The three groups contending for Bolshevik support – the delegates of the government of the Grand National Assembly in

Ankara, Enver and his fellow-exiles and Mustafa Suphi and his Moscow-line Turkish Communists, came face to face at the First Congress of the Peoples of the East which opened in Baku on 1 September 1920.

In April that year the Red Army had invaded Azerbaijan which became a Soviet Socialist Republic. But while the short-lived nationalist government of Azerbaijan was thus removed from power in Baku, 'bourgeois' nationalists were still in control of Armenia and Georgia to the west. Moreover, Bolshevik control was incomplete elsewhere in the Tsar's former possessions in Asia. The collapse of the Tsarist regime had brought to the fore indigenous revolutionaries in non-Russian communities. But these tended to be National Communists – nationalists first, Communists second. In the eyes of Moscow they were useful idiots, like Western apologists for the Bolsheviks, who could be liquidated at a later date. The purpose of the Baku Congress was to form an Eastern popular front of Moscow-line Communists, national Communists, radicals and anti-imperialists of various persuasions, in order to further the aims of the Bolsheviks.

The three competing groups of Turkish delegates kept in touch with each other, while eyeing each other with suspicion. Enver, who had formed a shadowy League of Islamic Revolutionaries, which existed largely in his imagination, took part as the self-appointed representative of the Muslims of North Africa. He had prepared a speech in which he argued that, had the Soviets been in power in 1914, he would have made common cause with them rather than with the Kaiser's Germany, but that, in any case, he had hastened the advent of the Russian Revolution by closing the Straits to the Allies in the First World War. However, Turkish Communists prevented Enver from reading his own speech, shouting: 'His place is not on the rostrum, but in the dock of a people's tribunal.' More realistically, Mustafa Kemal warned Enver against frightening the Bolsheviks with the spectre of Pan-Islam.[5]

Mustafa Kemal had to tread delicately to achieve his objective. He wanted to win material support from the Bolsheviks, while keeping them out of his country and at the same time regain territory lost to the Russians in 1878, which the Bolsheviks wanted for themselves. What he offered in return was Turkish acquiescence in the establishment of Soviet power in Azerbaijan, whatever was left of Armenia and a slightly reduced Georgia. To pacify the Bolsheviks further and preempt Turkey's own Marxist revolutionaries, he went through the motions of creating a 'people's government' in Ankara. In Marxist jargon, a 'people's republic' is an acceptable stage in the transition from capitalism to socialism. Having opened the National Assembly with elaborate Islamic ritual and proclaimed the nationalists' loyalty to the Sultan, Mustafa Kemal presented to his deputies the programme of the *people's government*, as he called his government on that occasion only – and then never again.[6] The programme, which set out the objective of 'liberating the Turkish nation from the domination of imperialism and capitalism ... with the help of God', was endorsed unanimously and enthusiastically by the National Assembly on 18 October 1920. It was, of course, never implemented, but it served its purpose domestically and internationally, and it has left some traces.

At home, the 'people's programme' helped Mustafa Kemal establish control over the People's Group, which consisted of some 60–70 Assembly members, and was the political wing of the Green Army. When the time came for Mustafa Kemal to form his own party, he called it the People's Party. After the proclamation of the republic, it became the Republican

People's Party, a name which it has retained to this day. For a long time, it ruled the country single-handed, but it has never achieved power single-handed in a free election. Abroad, there was of course no question of pulling the wool over the eyes of the Bolsheviks, but Mustafa Kemal's dealings with Moscow frightened the Principal Allies with the spectre of Communism.

Kâzım Karabekir, the nationalist commander in eastern Turkey, wrote in his memoirs that when he took up his command in May 1919, the British control officer, Colonel Alfred Rawlinson, confided in him that the Allies were in no position to stop the spread of Bolshevism by military means, for that would require calling up once again men who had just been demobilised. Karabekir thought that Rawlinson wanted him to provide an anti-Communist barrier in the Caucasus.[7] In the event Mustafa Kemal wrote off the Caucasus, while preventing the spread of Communism to Turkey.

In December 1920, after the Turkish nationalists and the Bolsheviks had partitioned the territory claimed by Armenian nationalists, Mustafa Suphi, the leader of Turkish Communists loyal to Moscow, left Baku for Turkey. As Karabekir did not allow him to enter Erzurum, he made his way to Trabzon. Harassed on the way and despairing of success, he found a boat for the return voyage to Bolshevik territory. He never made it. Thugs, organised by the Unionist boss of the guild of boatmen, embarked with him. Off the Turkish coast, they murdered Mustafa Suphi, his wife and 13 companions and threw their bodies overboard. Some time later, the perpetrators of the crime were themselves killed by the nationalist authorities. Ankara's relations with Moscow were not affected.

Just as Mustafa Kemal's diplomatic position was beginning to improve, the position of Greece weakened dramatically.

Venizelos had sought to capitalise on his illusory gains at Sèvres by calling a general election. On the eve of the elections, on 25 October 1920, King Alexander of Greece died of blood-poisoning after being bitten by a monkey in the palace grounds. Alexander had been brought to the throne as the unwilling successor to his father Constantine, an opponent of Greek entry into the war on the side of the Allies. Greeks living within the country's pre-war boundaries were war-weary. Venizelos, who knew this, employed questionable tactics to win the election. Greeks in the newly-acquired province of eastern Thrace, who were Venizelist to a man, were given the vote; so too were the armed forces, where Venizelist officers not only put pressure on their comrades, but falsified results. An opposition leader was murdered in Athens. Constantine's policy of neutrality appeared attractive in retrospect. Accused of tyranny, Venizelos was roundly beaten on 14 November by supporters of Constantine. On 2 December 1920, at French prompting, Britain, France and Italy issued a joint warning that 'the restoration to the throne of Greece of a King, whose disloyal attitude … towards the Allies during the war caused them great embarrassment and loss, could only be regarded by them as a ratification by Greece of his hostile acts'. In spite of this warning, the referendum held in Greece three days later yielded a massive vote for Constantine's return.[8]

Regime change could, at least in theory, have given Greece the opportunity to withdraw from Anatolia while trying to hang on to eastern Thrace. But withdrawal was not an easy option. Greeks who had been Ottoman subjects had compromised their position by siding with their country's enemies. What is more, Venizelos had convinced most metropolitan Greeks that he had settled 'the national question' – in other words that the annexation of 'Ionia' (western Anatolia) to Greece was an accomplished fact. Swayed by this unfounded belief, the new regime lost the opportunity to go for half a loaf. It was not the monkey's bite that changed the course of history. It was rather the decision of the new Greek regime under King Constantine to outbid Venizelos in expansionist zeal. Before long, the risks they had taken became clear on the ground.

The defeat of the Armenians and the understanding with Moscow allowed Mustafa Kemal to concentrate his forces on the western front against the Greeks. Karabekir stayed on in Erzurum, while the western front was entrusted to Colonel İsmet. In January 1921, Greek troops made a first attempt to move inland from the coastal areas they had occupied. Their main thrust was from the Bithynian plain, centred on Bursa, towards the town of Eskişehir, lying on the railway line between Istanbul and Ankara. On the edge of the Anatolian escarpment, near the small railway station of İnönü, they were met by İsmet's newly-assembled troops and thrown back. As a reward for his victory, İsmet was promoted to Brigadier by the National Assembly. The rank of one-star general carried with it the title of Pasha.

The Greeks claimed that their advance had been a probing manoeuvre rather than an offensive to defeat Turkish nationalists. Nevertheless, the setback had immediate political consequences. The Principal Allies called a conference in London to discuss a mutually acceptable revision of the Sèvres Treaty concluded four months earlier. They invited to it both the Istanbul and the Ankara governments, thus conferring a measure of recognition on the latter. As soon as the conference opened on 21 February 1921, the chief Ottoman delegate, Grand Vizier Tevfik Pasha, withdrew to the background, saying that the Turkish case would be presented by Bekir Sami, the Foreign Minister of the Ankara government. Predictably, the conference failed: the Greeks stood out for all their gains at Sèvres, Bekir Sami insisted on the National Pact – the integrity of Turkey within the 1918 armistice boundaries. But while the conference produced no results, on its margins Bekir Sami struck separate bargains with the Principal Allies, tempting them with economic concessions if they came to an agreement with Ankara. After his return, the bargains were repudiated by the Turkish National Assembly, and Bekir Sami resigned. But they widened the cracks in the laboriously constructed Allied united front.

While Bekir Sami was holding off and then tempting the Western Allies in London, another Turkish nationalist delegation was negotiating in Moscow. On 16 March, four days after the London conference had broken down, a Turkish-Soviet friendship agreement was signed in Moscow. A few months later, it was supplemented by a friendship agreement between Turkey, on the one hand, and, on the other, Georgia, Armenia and Azerbaijan, which had all become Soviet Socialist Republics. Turkey regained its pre-1878 eastern frontier, with the exception of the port of Batum which became the chief town of Ajaria (or Adjara), theoretically an autonomous republic within Georgia. Apart from fixing the eastern frontier of the Turkish state, the agreement also provided for Soviet aid in gold and weapons. It was to prove crucial in sustaining the military capacity of Turkish nationalists.

The first shipment of 1.5 million gold roubles arrived in December 1920. Others followed at regular intervals: another four million golden roubles, more than 33,000 rifles, 50 heavy guns (some left by the British), 300 machine-guns, etc.[9] Characteristically, the shipments came after a second Turkish military success. On 23 March 1921, the Greeks returned in force, trying once again to scale the escarpment near İnönü. At first they succeeded in storming some commanding heights. But a Turkish counter-attack on 31 March dislodged them from their gains. İsmet gave the news to Mustafa Kemal. From the peak of Metristepe, he reported, he could see the Greeks fleeing to the plain below. Turkish history records the victory as 'the second Battle of İnönü'. Mustafa Kemal congratulated İsmet with a Churchillian phrase which every Turkish school boy is meant to know by heart: *You have vanquished not just the enemy but also the ill fortune of our nation.*[10] Yet the country's destiny had to take another knock before it triumphed over adversity.

'You have vanquished not just the enemy but also the ill fortune of our nation.'

MUSTAFA KEMAL CONGRATULATING İSMET ON HIS VICTORY AT İNÖNÜ

As always, international politics then moved in response to the balance of forces on the ground. In May, the British, French and Italian High Commissioners in Istanbul, declared the Straits would be treated as a neutral zone. Given that the Sèvres Treaty had not been ratified, the Allies were officially still at war with the Ottoman state. But with their declaration of neutrality in the fighting between the armies of Constantine and those of Mustafa Kemal, the conflict which had started in 1914 between Turks and the Allies had been transformed into a Turkish-Greek war. This was underlined by the decision of the Italians in April and May to withdraw their occupation troops from Antalya and the area south of the Greek positions round İzmir. The Italians had arrived with supplies of food; they got on well with Turkish nationalists; and, finally, they left behind part of their equipment. The local Turkish population remembered them fondly.

The French were soon to follow suit. But, like the Bolsheviks, they wanted to see first whether the Turkish nationalists would hold their own in the war with the Greeks. However, even before the issue became clear on the western battlefields on Anatolia, the French commander in southern Turkey agreed to a 20-day armistice in May 1920. This was prompted by the capture by Turkish irregulars of a French detachment which had tried to hold a railway station in the Taurus mountains, north of Adana. As clashes then resumed between Turkish militias, commanded by regular officers, and French forces trying to hold the territory awarded to France under the Treaty of Sèvres, the French government sent an unofficial envoy to Ankara to reach an understanding with the nationalist authorities. The envoy, Henri Franklin-Bouillon, Chairman of the Senate Foreign Relations Committee, arrived in Ankara on 8 June 1921. He got on well with Mustafa Kemal, who guessed that France was willing to trade Turkish territory, north of the 1918 armistice lines, against Turkish acceptance of French rule in Syria. The French gave a preliminary sweetener by withdrawing their troops from Turkey's Black Sea coast where they were protecting French investments in Turkey's main coalfield. However, before a comprehensive deal was struck, France had to make sure that the Ankara government would survive the Greek onslaught in the west.

Rejecting the offer of mediation by Britain, France and Italy, the new Greek government reinforced its troops in Anatolia and launched a general offensive against the new and as yet untried Turkish army. Venizelos, who had moved to France after losing power in Athens, argued that by turning down the Allies' offer, his successors had led their country into diplomatic isolation. He had worked tirelessly, he said, to secure Britain's support for Greek territorial claims. Now that support had been compromised by Constantine's government.[11]

At first this did not seem important, as the Greek army made spectacular gains. İsmet was out-manoeuvred. He expected the Greeks to renew their attack from the west. But the main thrust came from the south, and threatened to cut off his headquarters in Eskişahir. The morale of the Turkish troops was severely shaken and large numbers deserted. It was a critical moment for the Turkish nationalists. After visiting the crumbling front, Mustafa Kemal decided to sacrifice territory in order to save the core of his army, and ordered it to withdraw to the east bank of the River Sakarya, the last natural barrier before Ankara. The Greeks pressed on rapidly from Eskişehir, advancing deeper into the treeless Anatolian plateau in the heat of summer. On 23 August, they crossed a tributary of the Sakarya river and attacked Turkish positions on the heights overlooking the east bank.

In Ankara, the civil servants of the embryonic nationalist administration prepared to leave their ramshackle offices in the caravanserais and dilapidated private houses of their Anatolian capital, and move with their papers to Kayseri, the most considerable city to the east. The families of deputies in the National Assembly joined in the evacuation. Greek aircraft appeared in the sky and dropped bombs on Ankara's railway station. But for all its unruly and fractious nature, the Assembly stood firm. 'Have we come here to fight or to run away like women?' asked a bearded Kurdish tribal leader, whose loyalty to the Turkish resistance movement is remembered to this day.[12] Faced with disaster, the deputies rallied round Mustafa Kemal. His place, they declared, was at the front in command of his troops. Mustafa Kemal agreed, but on condition that he was given extraordinary powers as commander-in-chief. It was a radical move, for under the Ottoman constitution it was the Sultan who was commander-in-chief. Nevertheless, the powers were granted, but only for a term of three months, renewable at the Assembly's discretion, and on condition that that they affected only the military conduct of the war and did not impinge on the Assembly's political prerogatives. These distinctions were lost to most Allied observers, who habitually referred to Mustafa Kemal as the nationalists' all-powerful 'generalissimo'.

Mustafa Kemal wasted no time in meeting the Greek threat. Promising the nation that the enemy would be *throttled in the inner sanctuary of the fatherland*,[13] he ordered the requisitioning of supplies – food, horses, peasant carts, clothes – from an already impoverished population. Providentially, the first supplies of Soviet weapons arrived in the nationalist-held ports of the Black Sea in the nick of time. They were hauled by bullock-cart along dirt tracks to the front, often driven by peasant women. Turkish schoolchildren are taught to remember the heroic participation of Turkish women in their country's defence.

A few months earlier, the nationalists had organised officer-training courses in Ankara. Freshly commissioned officers and cadets were thrown into the battle, which Mustafa Kemal directed from the small railway station of Polatlı, west of Ankara. Repeating their earlier successful manoeuvre, the Greeks tried to cut off Turkish forces by attacking them from the south, while keeping up the pressure from the west. They were better equipped than the Turks, but they fought in an inhospitable, alien environment. The arid plateau was ideal country for the cavalry, and the Turks made full use of it by harassing Greek lines of communications.

The Greek army fought well. It stormed the main heights

commanding the battlefield and advanced to within 30 miles of Ankara. Explaining the setback to the Assembly, Mustafa Kemal made the memorable statement: *We are not defending a line, but an area – the area that encompasses the whole of the fatherland. Not an inch of it is to be surrendered until it is drenched with the blood of our citizens.*[14] On 14 September he proclaimed a general mobilisation. This amounted to a final repudiation of the armistice agreement of 1918. Mustafa Kemal's strategy worked. The Greeks could not sustain their offensive. Sensing this, the Turkish army launched a counter-attack, forcing the Greek command to order a withdrawal to the west of the Sakarya river. Turkish troops were too exhausted to pursue them, and the Greeks returned to their starting point at Eskişehir, destroying everything in their path: villages, bridges, and the railway line to Ankara. It was a foretaste of what was to happen in much of western Turkey.

'We are not defending a line, but an area – the area that encompasses the whole of the fatherland. Not an inch of it is to be surrendered until it is drenched with the blood of our citizens.'

MUSTAFA KEMAL AT THE BATTLE OF SAKARYA

On 17 September it became clear that the Turks had succeeded in throwing back the Greek offensive. The following day, Mustafa Kemal returned to Ankara. On 19 September a grateful Assembly promoted him to the rank of Field Marshal, and awarded him the title of Gazi. Its literal meaning is 'warrior for the faith (of Islam)', while in current usage it designates old combatants in general (soldiers who are killed are remembered as *şehit*, or martyrs), and heroic commanders, in particular.

The Battle of Sakarya is remembered in Turkey as 'the

officers' battle'. The army of the National Assembly had some 5,000 officers in all. Of them 300 were killed and a thousand wounded in the battle, as they led soldiers demoralised by the retreat from Eskişehir, and raw peasant recruits who had just joined the ranks. Total Turkish casualties of 3,700 dead and 18,000 wounded roughly matched the Greeks' losses.[15] But Mustafa Kemal had greater reserves of manpower, and his fellow-countrymen had their backs to the wall and pulled together, while Greek opinion was sharply divided on the wisdom of the invasion of Anatolia.

Mustafa Kemal was not the first Turkish commander to become known popularly as Gazi Pasha: Osman Pasha the heroic defender of the Ottoman fortress of Plevna on the Danube in the Russo-Turkish war of 1877–8, is remembered as Gazi Osman Pasha. Similarly, Edhem Pasha, the victorious commander of Ottoman troops in the war with Greece in 1897, is known as Gazi Edhem Pasha, and boys born to families of Turkish refugees from the island of Crete (for which the war was fought), are taken to venerate his tomb after they are circumcised. Mustafa Kemal's distinction was to receive the title from a democratic parliamentary assembly.

King Constantine had staked his throne on the success of the policy of waging war to the finish against the Ankara government. He had arrived in İzmir before the offensive began. It was not a successful visit: the Greek occupation authorities restricted his movements for fear of an attempt on his life; and the King was not impressed by the local Greeks who, he felt, expected their kinsmen from continental 'old' Greece to win the country for them. But Constantine's harshest remarks were reserved for the Turks. Moving to the newly-occupied town of Eskişehir, where his younger brother Prince Andrew (the father of the Duke of Edinburgh) commanded an army corps, he wrote: 'It is extraordinary how little civilised the Turks are ... It is high time they disappeared once more and went back into the interior of Asia whence they came.'[16] But the Turks had no intention of disappearing, and, as far as civilisation was concerned, as Constantine had to admit himself, both sides fought each other with the greatest cruelty. The term 'ethnic cleansing' had not been invented at the time, but the reality was practised by both sides. Greeks drove Turks out of their villages in their zone of occupation; Turks deported Greeks from the coastlands they controlled. The shelling of Turkey's harbours on the Black Sea by Greek warships provided an excuse for the deportation of Black Sea Greeks, but the long-term aim of the deportation was to pre-empt Greek-Armenian plans to establish a Christian state of Pontus.

The deportation worried the representative of the area in the National Assembly in Ankara. Well-to-do Greeks and Turks lived side by side in some coastal towns. One deputy asked that Turkish property should be protected from the looting which inevitably followed the deportation of Greek householders. The practice of looting and then setting fire to the houses of the ethnic adversary was widespread during the long process of the dissolution of the Ottoman Empire. The deliberate destruction which the present generation witnessed in former Yugoslavia had well-established historical precedents. Militarily, Mustafa Kemal's success at the Battle of Sakarya was the turning point of the war. Unable to launch another offensive, the Greeks began to blame each other as they sought a way to cut short the conflict. It was a royalist, German-trained general, Ioannis Metaxas, the future dictator of Greece, who was the first to offer a realistic diagnosis. 'It is only superficially,' he said, 'a question of the Treaty of Sèvres. It is really a question of the dissolution of Turkey and the establishment of our state on Turkish soil … And the Turks realise what we want. If they had no national feeling, perhaps such a policy would be possible. But they have proved that they have, not a religious, but a national feeling. And they mean to fight for their freedom and independence.'[17]

Politically, success at Sakarya saved Mustafa Kemal's position both domestically and internationally. As the outcome was being decided, Enver waited on the Soviet side of the border in Batum, ready to bid for the leadership of Turkish resistance if Mustafa Kemal fell by the wayside. After Sakarya, Enver gave up any hope of returning and made for Central Asia. Instead of joining with the Bolsheviks against the British, he drifted – without realising what he was doing – into the ranks of the *Basmachi* or raiders, a disorganised popular movement of local Muslims who resisted the imposition of Soviet rule in Central Asia. It was his last adventure. He was killed in what is today the independent republic of Tajikistan, when the Red Army caught up with his band of irregulars and wiped it out. Having gambled with the lives of millions of his countrymen and lost, he gambled with his own life and lost again. Turks today remember his dashing courage and his patriotism, however wrong-headed. But for Mustafa Kemal he served as the counter-exemplar, who demonstrated the perils of adventurism.

Moscow understood that Mustafa Kemal had no time for Pan-Islamic adventures, and caused him no difficulties when he got rid of Communists in his own country. Arrests of Communists in Anatolia began early in 1921 when Mustafa Kemal's army won its first successes at İnönü. After Sakarya, in October that year, Mustafa Kemal formed his own official Communist Party and ordered some of his generals to register as members. The official party was not admitted to the Communist International, but it served its purpose in weeding out such Turkish Communists as would not join it.

The most famous was Nazım Hikmet, Turkey's best-known

and best-loved modern poet. Typically, he came from a family of high officials of Polish origin. He was greeted as a hero in Anatolia when he joined the nationalist movement in January 1921. But his romantic revolutionary zeal could not be accommodated in Ankara, and he was sent off to teach in a provincial school. Disappointed, Nazım Hikmet slipped off to Moscow where he moved in the circle of Mayakovsky, the leading Russian revolutionary poet. He returned to Turkey after the nationalist victory in 1923, and was imprisoned time and again. He finally fled behind the Iron Curtain in 1951, just as Turkey became involved in the Cold War on the side of the West. Nazım Hikmet died in Moscow in 1963, leaving behind a body of work which has changed the course of Turkish poetry.

The most important diplomatic consequence of the Battle of Sakarya was the conclusion on 20 October 1921 of an agreement with France. Officially called an '*accord*', it was in fact a preliminary separate peace treaty, which established the frontier between Turkey and French-ruled Syria. In exchange for French evacuation of southern Turkey, Turkey gave up – provisionally, as it happened – the district of İskenderun/Alexandretta. But the accord promised to establish a special administration there, which would protect the rights of its Turkish-speaking inhabitants. The Turkish government remained loyal to its implicit promise to desist from any interference in the internal affairs of Syria. Having frightened the French with the prospect of cooperation between Turkish and Arab nationalists, Mustafa Kemal turned away from the Arabs. As the last commander of Ottoman troops which had faced the disloyalty of Arab nationalists, he owed them nothing, and least of all to the Hashemites, who had accepted British gold to harass the Turks. The French were to prove less meticulous than the Turks in carrying out their commitments. While anti-French Arab nationalists were denied facilities in Turkey, Kurdish exiles from Turkey, grouped round a tribal dynasty, were allowed to keep the feeble flame of Kurdish nationalism alive in Syria.

Apart from a free hand in Syria, France wanted to safeguard its network of schools, most of which were run by Catholic teaching orders in Istanbul. As ever, the promotion of French culture ranked high in French foreign policy. Kemal, who had been moulded by that culture, even if it was at second hand, did not object, for in his eyes, and in the eyes of most of his companions, France represented civilisation – not Western civilisation, but the one single civilisation of mankind. It followed that far from obstructing the development of an independent Turkey, French culture promoted it. However, Kemal resisted French pressure for economic privileges. France had been the major investor in the Ottoman Empire, including British-ruled Egypt, and it fought hard to keep the regime of capitulations, which allowed foreigners extraterritorial rights. The Ankara accord made no mention of the capitulations. They were left for the final peace treaty between Turkey and the Allies.

The British were thus left as the sole defenders of the Greeks in Turkey. But cracks appeared in the British position too. While Lloyd George remained totally committed to the Greek nationalist cause, in spite of the fall from power in Athens of his fatal friend Venizelos, the Foreign Office under Curzon sought to lessen the damage done to British interests by Lloyd George's policy. The British High Commissioner in the Ottoman capital, Sir Horace Rumbold, believed that the future struggle for influence in Turkey would be fought between Britain and France. 'If this struggle comes,' he claimed, 'it will not be so much owing to any action taken by England but rather the direct result of French jealousy.'[18] Doubts in London were reinforced by the stalwart opposition of the India Office to any step that might antagonise Indian Muslims and shake their loyalty to the British Raj. While civilian politicians argued and intrigued among themselves, it was the military who acted to avoid the risk of a clash with Turkish nationalists. In July 1921, on the eve of the Turkish victory at Sakarya, the Allied commander-in-chief in Turkey, General Sir Charles ('Tim') Harington, agreed to meet Mustafa Kemal on board a British warship off the Turkish-held Black Sea port of İnebolu. The plan had been hatched by a demobilised British officer, Major James Henry, who was trying to win a mining concession in Anatolia. He suggested to the Turks that the British were keen on such a meeting, while telling the British military that the Turks wanted it. The intrigue fell through. Told that Harington was willing to meet him, Mustafa Kemal replied that he would come only if the British general agreed in advance to the complete liberation of the national territory and Turkey's unqualified independence in the political, financial, economic, judicial and religious spheres.[19] Nevertheless, even if the initiative failed, it showed that the British military were ready to establish contact with Turkish nationalists.

In February 1922, the Ankara government sent its foreign minister Yusuf Kemal, who had succeeded Bekir Sami, to put its case directly to the French and British governments. On his way to France, Yusuf Kemal called on the British High Commissioner in Istanbul, and impressed him with his determination to accept nothing short of the sovereign independence of Turkey within the 1918 armistice lines. When Sir Horace Rumbold suggested that territorial concessions might be necessary, he replied that 'compromise must not always be at the expense of Turkey'.[20] At the end of March, the British, French and Italian foreign ministers meeting in Paris proposed an immediate armistice, followed by negotiations for a new peace treaty. The proposal fell on deaf ears: the Turks demanded a full Greek withdrawal as soon as the armistice was concluded; the Greeks turned this down, believing that the Turks were incapable of turning them out of İzmir and eastern Thrace.

The Greeks sought desperately to avert the disaster threatening their Anatolian adventure. But their attempt to force the issue resulted in uniting all the Allies against them. In mid-July 1922, the Greeks threatened to march on Istanbul in the belief that possession of the Ottoman capital would give them the leverage to impose their terms on the Turks. Portraits of King Constantine appeared in the front windows of Greek shops in Istanbul, surmounted by the one word '*Erchetai!*' – 'He is coming!'. But Constantine did not come to regain the city lost to the Turks by his namesake in 1453. For once, the Principal Allies acted in unison, and reinforced their warning to the Greeks to stay out of the neutral zone by assembling their troops and warships to resist a Greek march on Istanbul by force if necessary. The Greeks stopped in their tracks, having diverted to no purpose troops needed in western Anatolia for the final battle with the Turks.

Instead of counselling caution, Lloyd George hastened to undo the effect of the Allies' belated show of firmness. 'We are not allowing the Greeks to wage the war with their full strength,' he declared in the House of Commons on 4 August. 'We cannot allow that sort of thing to go on indefinitely, in the hope that the Kemalists entertain, that they will at last exhaust this little country, whose men have been under arms for ten or twelve years ... and which has not indefinite resources.'[21] But allow 'that sort of thing' was precisely what the Allies, including Britain, did. To paraphrase Henry Kissinger, one cannot expect a Great Power to commit suicide (or even to endanger its interests) in defence of an unwise ally.

As the Greek advance on Istanbul was being halted, the Greek proconsul in İzmir, Aristeidis Stergiadis, tried another way to lighten the burden. On 31 July he issued a proclamation saying that 'the work of liberation' would be continued 'by the liberating people itself', in other words by the locals and not by the Greek government. The administration of the area held by Greeks troops under the terms of the Sèvres Treaty would be reorganised accordingly.[22] But autonomy for Ionia made no sense. There were no Ionians, as there had been in classical antiquity, but only Greeks and Turks, and they were no longer able to live under the same roof. As the Greeks looked for outside help to hang on to their gains, the Turks took on 'the work of liberation' for themselves. The only effect of Stergiadis's initiative was to demoralise Greek troops even further, for in effect they were being asked to fight for territory which was about to be given up in any case.

In Ankara, Mustafa Kemal came under increasing pressure to take the offensive. Nearly a year had passed since the Greeks had been stopped at the Battle of Sakarya. The Turkish national army had replenished its ranks with newly-commissioned officers and recruits, and its arsenals with arms left behind by the French and the Italians, in addition to earlier shipments from Russia. What was the Commander-in-Chief waiting for? The answer was that Mustafa Kemal was keenly aware of the poverty of his domestic resources. His government controlled the most backward part of the country, without industry and with precious few skills. The new strength of the nationalists could easily be dissipated in an ill-planned operation. Mustafa Kemal wanted to be sure that he would be able to deliver a decisive blow, and before that to exhaust all possibilities of achieving his objective without further destruction and bloodshed. He proceeded cautiously. He inspected the front in July under cover of a football match between two army teams, which he watched in the company of his commanders. Having satisfied himself that his army was ready, he returned to Ankara and persuaded his ministers to minute their agreement with his decision to launch an offensive. Failure would have not only military but also political consequences. He tried to guard against both. To preserve complete secrecy, an announcement was put out that the Commander-in-Chief would be staying in Ankara to host a tea party at his residence. Then all communications were cut between Anatolia and the outside world.

An army of 225,000 Greeks were deployed against 208,000 Turks along a front which stretched from the shores of the Sea of Marmara in the north to the valley of the River Menderes (Meander), south of İzmir. Like other successful generals, Mustafa Kemal took the strategically sound risk of concentrating most of his forces on a narrow sector, leaving the rest of his front uncovered. It was the strategy of the single knock-out blow, which became known as the *blitzkrieg*. He targeted his offensive on the pivot of the Greek line, the peaks which dominated the town of Afyon on the main railway line from Istanbul. The Afyon salient was where the Greek front-line changed direction from north-south to east-west, and was therefore open to attack from two sides. The main blow was delivered from the south to the right flank of the fortified mountain positions held by the Greeks. The intention was to cut them off from their rear base in İzmir, where the Greek

Commander-in-Chief General George Hatzianestis had his headquarters on board a ship. Hatzianestis was an eccentric disciplinarian, who, it was rumoured, believed that his legs were made of glass and could break at any moment. But it was his army that broke.

The issue was decided in the sector chosen by Mustafa Kemal. On 25 August 1922, he joined his battle headquarters on the 6,000-foot high peak of Kocatepe. The following day, the Turks let loose an artillery barrage on the Greek positions on the peaks facing them. Then the Turkish troops advanced, climbing up the slopes against determined Greek resistance. The first day the Greek lines held. But Turkish determination was not dented. A Turkish colonel committed suicide because he could not keep his promise to capture a position as quickly as he had promised. *It is not because I approve his action that I am telling you this*, Mustafa Kemal said in his report to Parliament a few days later. *Such behaviour is unacceptable. But I wanted to illustrate the spirit in which our officers and our commanders discharged their duty.*[23]

The Turkish breakthrough came the following day, 27 August. Almost immediately, Greek morale collapsed. Their officers were bitterly divided into two rival camps, as Venizelists tried to undermine supporters of King Constantine. Troops had been exposed to Communist agitation about the imperialist nature of the war. Soldiers did not trust their officers, and the officers did not trust other ranks – or each other. Greek units retreating from their positions on the hills surrounding Afyon lost contact with each other. Many were surrounded. The retreat which started at Afyon extended to the whole front as far north as the Sea of Marmara. On 1 September, Mustafa Kemal issued his famous order: *Armies, your immediate objective is the Mediterranean. Forward!*[24]

On 2/3 September, two Greek corps commanders surrendered when they found they had fallen into a trap. One of them, General Trikoupis, learned after his capture that he had been appointed commander of the entire front.

It took Turkish frontline troops six days to cover the 250 miles from Afyon to İzmir. As the Greeks fled to the coast, they set fire to towns and villages, destroying all that lay on their path. Units which managed to make it, slipped through İzmir, leaving behind its terror-stricken Greek, Armenian and foreign citizens, and embarked on ships waiting off the Çeşme peninsula further west. On 9 September, Turkish troops entered İzmir. Mustafa Kemal made his official entry the following day. Three days later there was not a Greek soldier left anywhere in Anatolia, except for prisoners. A few days later there was almost nothing left of İzmir – or more accurately of Levantine Smyrna – and of its non-Muslim inhabitants.

There were sporadic incidents of violence as Turkish troops advanced through the prosperous suburbs, where English and other European merchants had their villas, and entered the city. The troops were commanded by Nurettin Pasha, known as 'bearded Nurettin', who was notorious for his cruelty. He had been in command of the Ottoman troops which had besieged General Townshend's force in Kut in 1915 during the Mesopotamian campaign, but had been relieved of his command by Von der Goltz, the German officer in overall command, before the British surrendered. At the end of the First World War, he was commander of the Turkish garrison in İzmir until the Allies insisted on his replacement just before the Greek landing. The Ankara government appointed him commander of the Central Army, whose task was to keep control of the nationalists' rear. It was this army which forced the Greek civilian population out of their homes along the

Black Sea coast and then went on to suppress Kurdish risings. This was accompanied by so much bloodshed and destruction that the Grand National Assembly wanted to have Nurettin court-martialled. But Mustafa Kemal was short of commanders and saved him from the wrath of the Assembly, transferring him to the command of the First Army under İsmet Pasha's overall command on the western front.

As commandant of a captured city, Nurettin had the duty of ensuring law and order in İzmir. But when the Greek Archbishop Chrysostom visited him to plead for the safety of his community, Nurettin handed him over to a mob of vengeful Muslims who tore the unfortunate prelate to pieces. Admittedly, it was difficult to restrain soldiers who had seen the destruction wrought by the retreating Greeks, and who found themselves in a prosperous city after years of hardship and grinding poverty. But no effort was made to prevent revenge killings and looting. And, as usual, once looting started fires followed, destroying the lives and property of ethnic adversaries.

The great fire of İzmir started in the Armenian quarter. In all, 20–25,000 buildings were burned down and an area of 2.5 million square metres was devastated.[25] It was later claimed that the trouble was caused by Armenian resistance and by explosions of ammunition hidden in Armenian homes. Hatred between the Turks and the Armenians was intense, and only the strictest measures could have prevented a murderous confrontation. But instead of reining in ethnic hatred, Nurettin encouraged it. He did nothing to stop the killings and looting. The depleted city fire service was incapable of controlling the fire which engulfed the town right up to the waterfront. Only the poverty-stricken Turkish quarter on the heights round the citadel, the Jewish quarter and the immediate surroundings of the French consulate near the quayside were spared, suggesting that disloyal fellow-subjects of the Sultan were deliberately targeted.

Terrified Greeks, Armenians and other Christians crowded the quays, begging to be taken on board Allied warships and transports anchored in the harbour. At first, Allied officers tried to restrict evacuation to their nationals, but as the harbour filled with the bodies of refugees who had thrown themselves on the mercy of Allied seamen, they had to accept on board civilians of any nationality, including Ottoman subjects. Within a few days 213,000 men, women and children were evacuated from the ruined city and carried to safety on board Allied warships and merchantmen.[26] It was a remarkable achievement.

The population of Levantine Smyrna was estimated at some 250,000 before the war. Swollen by refugees from the countryside, it was probably nearer 300,000 when Turkish troops regained the city in September 1922. Non-Muslims, the vast majority Greeks, accounted for over 60 per cent of the city's population,[27] while, as was usual in Anatolia, Muslims were more numerous in the countryside. There were more Greeks in the city of Smyrna than in Athens, and they were much more prosperous, having grown rich on the trade of this long-established gateway to Western Anatolia with its large, safe and easily accessible harbour. Since the end of the 19th century, British-built and owned railways linked Smyrna with the fertile river valleys which provided an easy route to the interior. Britain was the main destination of exports valued at some £4 million before the war and the main source of imports worth £3 million.[28] Smyrna merchants sold carpets, dried fruit, tobacco, liquorice and other farm produce, and imported foreign cloth and other manufactured goods.

Non-Muslim merchants dominated trade, and non-Muslims monopolised the professions and manned most skilled trades. Their forced exodus was a tragedy – the term humanitarian disaster had not yet gained currency – which unrolled before the eyes of the outside world. It engendered feelings of hatred, which are only now beginning to subside. It changed the character of a great merchant port. But after a lengthy interval of reconstruction, the prosperity of İzmir revived and gradually came to surpass its former glories.

While the Armenians scattered all over the world, with France and America their favourite destinations, most Greeks were resettled in Greece – in shanty-towns around Athens or on property formerly owned by Muslims in Salonica and elsewhere. Salonica, which mirrors İzmir/Smyrna on the Greek shore of the Aegean, had suffered a disastrous fire two years earlier, when 9,500 buildings were destroyed and over 70,000 people lost their homes, with the Jewish quarter being worst affected.[29] Later, these refugee settlements in metropolitan Greece were to become a breeding-ground of radical resentment which culminated in the civil war after the Second World War. But politics did not absorb all the energy of the refugees, some of whom, such as the shipping tycoon Aristotle Onassis, applied their skills in their new environment and became rich international entrepreneurs. It was not only commercial talent which found a new home. Smyrna was the birthplace of Adamantios Korais, the father of the Greek Enlightenment, and the rich cultural life of Greek Smyrniots transplanted to foreign soil nourished the genius of Maria Callas, along with other artists and writers.

Just as Greece profited from the energy of Smyrniot refugees, so İzmir owed its revival largely to Muslim refugees from the Balkans, in general, and Salonica in particular, who provided the elite of the new Turkish city. Its revival was at first slow. On the eve of the Second World War, the authorities encouraged the revival by organising the annual İzmir International Fair, held in a park planted in an area destroyed by fire. Even so, the population of the city in 1945 at 200,000 inhabitants was still below its 1919 level. Growth then exploded, as migrants from the interior arrived in their thousands to profit from the city's natural advantages. Today some three million people live in the İzmir metropolitan area – ten times as many as in Salonica. There are four universities, smart shops, luxury hotels to cater for business travellers and the millions of tourists who visit the area, and a thriving civic culture.

Levantine Smyrna was a European enclave on the Turkish shore of the Aegean. Its destruction has given rise to a great European city integrated with the rest of Turkey. Mustafa Kemal prepared the ground for this transformation by holding Turkey's first economic congress in the devastated city in February 1923, even before peace was signed, and encouraging native free enterprise. But he also valued the lively Mediterranean lifestyle of the city which his army had regained. Legend has it that as soon as he set foot in İzmir on 10 September he made for a Greek-owned restaurant with a view of the sea and ordered a bottle of *rakı*, his favourite anis-flavoured Turkish spirit. *Did King Constantine come here to enjoy a glass of* rakı*?* he asked the proprietor. 'No, Pasha,' replied the Greek. *Then why did he bother to occupy İzmir?* quipped Mustafa Kemal. In September 1920, the National Assembly in Ankara banned the consumption of alcoholic drinks. But this concession to Islamic sentiment did not cramp Mustafa Kemal's style: he was to die of cirrhosis of the liver at the age of 57. The ban was lifted in 1924, after the war was won.

The occupation of İzmir by the Greeks had mobilised Turkish resistance to the partition plans of the Allies. The city was now to play an important part also in the consummation of the victory of Turkish nationalists. It was from İzmir that Mustafa Kemal decided to move Turkish troops north to press against the British-held perimeter of the neutral zone of the Straits.

During the four years which followed his return from the Syrian front at the end of the First World War, Mustafa Kemal had done his best to avoid a direct clash with the British, while he fought British protégés at home and abroad. He also encouraged contacts, however indirect and tentative, to convey his message that British policy towards his country was wrong-headed, and that if Britain accepted Turkey's full independence within the 1918 armistice lines, he would be only too happy to be its friend in the region and beyond. He had explained his position at a secret session of the Assembly as early as 24 April 1920, the day after its official opening in Ankara. *Our nation is not opposed to the English*, he said. *On the contrary it acknowledges and respects them as the greatest, the most just, most civilised and humane nation in the world ... But after the armistice, the British entered our capital, and after establishing close contact with our people, they oversaw and backed the Greek occupation of the province of Aydın [İzmir] ... So we said 'Do something to correct [your policy] and our nation will once again turn to you [in friendship]'.*[30] Lloyd George was deaf to the message, but the British military were more receptive. And it was the attitude of the British (and Allied) Commander-in-Chief in Istanbul, General Harington, which prevented an armed clash between British and Turkish troops in September 1922.

Mustafa Kemal's aim in sending his troops to the perimeter

of British positions at Çanakkale (Chanak), the fortress on the Asian side of the entrance to the Dardanelles, was to ensure that Istanbul and eastern Thrace up to the 1914 frontier came under the control of his government. With the exception of clashes with French occupation forces south of the Taurus mountains, officially attributed to popular resistance, he had succeeded from May 1919 onwards in achieving his objectives one by one without fighting British, French or Italian troops. Now, once again, he used the threat of force to avoid recourse to it. And once again the tactic worked. British policy changed in the way that Mustafa Kemal had suggested right at the beginning.

'Our nation is not opposed to the English. On the contrary, it acknowledges and respects them as the greatest, the most just, most civilised and humane nation in the world.'
MUSTAFA KEMAL

The painful, noisy and messy – but, in the last resort, effective – change in British policy was the essence of the Chanak Crisis, as it came to be called, which lasted for barely a month from mid-September to mid-October 1922. And it was not only British policy towards Turkey that changed. So too did the governments in London and Athens. The crisis affected also the relationship between London and the Dominions: the refusal of most of the Dominions to back a new conflict (New Zealand and Newfoundland were the two exceptions) marked the growing independence of the constituent parts of the British Empire. The change was bloodless for the British, bloody in Athens. But what came out of the Chanak Crisis was the birth of a new dispensation in the Near East, a dispensation which has lasted to our day. The peace treaty which was signed in Lausanne nine months later confirmed the outcome of the Chanak Crisis. Fortunately for the world, the crisis did not end, but merely interrupted, the career of one of the enemies of change, Winston Churchill.

Churchill was to describe his position with characteristic elegance. 'Defeat is a nauseating draught,' he wrote, 'and that the victors in the greatest of all wars should gulp it down was not readily to be accepted. So having done my utmost for three years to procure a friendly peace with Mustapha Kemal and the withdrawal of the Greeks from Asia Minor, and having consistently opposed my friend the Prime Minister upon this issue, I now found myself wholeheartedly upon his side in resisting the consequences of the policy which I had condemned.'[31] Churchill was an imperialist. He resisted the independence of India. He guided the British Empire through the perils of the Second World War and presided over its transformation into the Commonwealth. He believed in the benefits of empire for all its subjects, just as the French believed in their civilising mission in their empire and beyond. But Mustafa Kemal too had been a loyal servant of his empire, the Ottoman state, and had fought hard on three continents to defend its frontiers. He also believed passionately in the value of the civilisation which had developed in the West, and which Western empires were propagating throughout the world. His success in establishing a Turkish national state on the ruins of the Ottoman Empire, in the teeth of Western opposition, did not blind him to the merits of British or French administration for people who were as yet incapable of achieving and sustaining civilised self-rule.

It was natural to fear for the safety of Istanbul, the cosmopolitan capital of the Ottoman state in the wake of the humanitarian disaster which had just stricken Levantine Smyrna. Non-Muslims, particularly non-Muslim Ottoman subjects, as well as those Muslims who had sided with the Sultan and pinned their faith on the Allies, were terrified at the prospect of the forcible entry of the Turkish nationalist army into their city. But although Allied officials in Istanbul were keenly aware of these fears, the main concerns of the British government were different.

There was, of course, the prestige of the victors to be considered. But geopolitics was more important. Control of the Straits had been achieved at the cost of great sacrifices in the First World War. Freedom of navigation was important for the great trading powers of the West, although less important now that the Bolsheviks had seized control of Russia, which ceased to be a significant trading partner of the West. Now the pressing need was for a bulwark against Bolshevism. Mustafa Kemal had cooperated with the Bolsheviks, while Venizelos had sent Greek troops to Odessa to help the White Russian counter-revolutionaries. For the British government in particular, the rise of the Bolsheviks revived the fear of Russian expansion which had inspired the policy of supporting the Turks throughout the 19th century. That policy had been abandoned as the Kaiser's Germany came to present a greater threat to British (and French) interests, and, of course, as the Young Turks threw in their lot with the Germans. Lloyd George had been persuaded by Venizelos that Greece could replace Turkey as the defender of the northern frontier of the Near East, an area long important to Britain as it lay across the route to India. Moreover, British and French rule newly established in the Arab lands had to be defended. But the defeat of the Greeks by Turkish nationalists had disproved the arguments of Venizelos. It was no use blaming the French, the Italians, the soldiers, the opposition and the press at home, as Lloyd George did, for the defeat of the Greeks and, consequently, of his policy. The policy had failed and an alternative had to be found.

When Turkish troops entered the neutral zone and pressed against the British positions round Çanakkale, the first reaction of the British government was to reinforce the troops on the ground and the warships patrolling the Straits. As there were no reserves available, appeals were sent to the Dominions to help guard the positions for which thousands of Anzacs had died. But Australia was unwilling to send its men back to Gallipoli. In fact none of the Allies was willing to fight the Turks.

This became clear when Curzon went to Paris to meet the French Prime Minister Raymond Poincaré. 'It was both a moral and physical impossibility for France to resist the Turks if they advanced,' Poincaré told Curzon, adding 'French public opinion would not admit of a shot being fired against the Turk.' Curzon burst into tears, complaining: 'Never in my life have I had to endure such speeches'. It made no difference. On 23 September, ten days after the arrival of Turkish troops outside Çanakkale, Poincaré, Curzon and Count Sforza sent a joint note to Ankara which went a long way towards meeting Mustafa Kemal's objectives. The note declared that the Allies 'viewed with favour' the desire of Turkey to recover eastern Thrace, including Edirne (Adrianople), and the Turks could have Istanbul after the peace was signed. As a first step, they suggested a meeting between the Allied Generals and Mustafa Kemal – at Mudanya, south of the Sea of Marmara, or İzmit on the eastern approaches to Istanbul.[32]

Mustafa Kemal wanted – and needed – a more precise commitment. On 23 September, the same day that the Principal Allies sent their joint note to Mustafa Kemal, there was a military coup in Athens. King Constantine was forced to abdicate and a junta of Venizelist colonels seized power. Just as Constantine's return to the throne in 1920 had not halted the Greek invasion of Anatolia, but, on the contrary, had channelled more resources into it, so now the revolutionary colonels sought to prove their patriotic credentials by assembling troops in Thrace and hanging on at least to their country's gains in European Turkey. In the circumstances, the Allies' promise 'to look with favour' on the restoration of Turkey's 1914 frontier in Europe was not sufficient. What Mustafa Kemal wanted was for the Allies themselves to evict the Greeks. Urged by some nationalist politicians to extend the war to Europe, he replied that he would not sacrifice a single Turkish gendarme for an object he could achieve by peaceful means. Mustafa Kemal's popularity with his troops was well merited.

The Chanak crisis showed also Mustafa Kemal's mastery of a very modern skill. Right from the beginning of his career, he had realised the importance of the press and made every effort to make friends of journalists. However, he also made sure that it was he and not the press who set the political agenda. During the First World War, Enver, the country's virtual military dictator, had deprived him of publicity. When Mustafa Kemal returned to Istanbul in November 1918 after the signature of the armistice, one of his first steps was to start a newspaper which would propagate his fame and his views. The newspaper (which was managed by Fethi [Okyar], Mustafa Kemal's main political ally in the capital) was called *Minber* ('The Pulpit'). It served Mustafa Kemal's purpose in presenting him as a safe candidate for his crucial appointment to Anatolia.

Almost immediately after his move to Ankara, Mustafa Kemal set up a press agency. Called the Anatolian Agency and staffed by professional journalists, it helped raise morale at home by disseminating news and comment which favoured the nationalists, and made their views known abroad. But securing the friendship of foreign correspondents was a more effective way of influencing public opinion in countries where they had greater credibility. Here Mustafa Kemal was fortunate in his choice of contacts. The French journalist Berthe Georges Gaulis visited him in Ankara and her friendly articles earned her the thanks of the Turkish National Assembly. Later her books made Mustafa Kemal's reforms known and appreciated in the West. But it was the attention that Mustafa Kemal had paid to a British correspondent, George Ward Price of the *Daily Mail*, which was to prove particularly beneficial during the Chanak Crisis. Ward Price had made his name as a war reporter when still in his mid-twenties during the Balkan Wars of 1912–13. Mustafa Kemal first met him in Istanbul in 1918 when he tried to persuade him of his friendly feelings towards Britain. Ward Price's reports from Turkey made him no friends among British officialdom. In the words of Neville Henderson, British Deputy High Commissioner in Istanbul, Ward Price 'dropped like a vulture from the sky' on a news story.[33] But what mattered was the effect of his reports on the editorial policy of his paper. Even although Ward Price praised the mettle of British troops which faced the Turks at Chanak, the *Daily Mail* concluded that Churchill's efforts to mobilise the Dominions against the Turks were 'bordering upon insanity'. On 21 September, the newspaper came out with the headline 'Get out of Chanak'.

Sir Horace Rumbold, the British High Commissioner, was enraged by the press which, he believed, had readily supported the Turkish nationalist cause. *The Daily Mail*, he wrote, was 'beneath contempt'. *The Morning Post* 'shuts its eyes to the bestialities of the Turks and slobbers over the French who don't deserve it.' As for the French Press, it 'seems to be in the grip of the International financier or Jew who only cares for French financial interests and nothing else'.[34] The self-righteous diplomat raged in vain. Mustafa Kemal's handling of the press helped him achieve his objectives.

Sir Horace Rumbold (1869–1941), British diplomat, dealt with Ottoman peace overtures in 1918 when he was minister in Switzerland. Appointed High Commissioner in Istanbul/ Constantinople in 1920, he did not develop the slightest sympathy for the Turks. Curzon nevertheless chose him as his chief assistant at Lausanne, where he became chief British delegate during the second stage of the conference leading up to the signature of the peace treaty. As ambassador in Berlin, he witnessed the Nazis' rise to power. His assistant in Istanbul, Sir Neville Henderson, became the last British ambassador in Berlin before the outbreak of the Second World War.

On 29 September, General Harington was instructed to deliver an ultimatum to the Ankara government demanding that Turkish troops should withdraw from the neutral zone immediately. If they did not, the British would attack them. Fortunately, General Harington was as determined as Mustafa Kemal to avoid a resumption of hostilities. Instead of delivering the ultimatum, he continued negotiations with the Turkish nationalists' representative in Istanbul. The Greek fleet, he said, had been withdrawn from the Sea of Marmara on 27 September 'under the strongest British pressure'. The French unofficial representative, the indefatigable Franklin Bouillon, reported that the Ankara government was prepared to negotiate an armistice leading to a peace settlement. Harington called him 'a perfect curse', but believed that if the Frenchman helped the two sides to sit round a conference table, he would have performed a useful service.[35]

On 1 October, the Ankara government agreed to meet

Allied representatives in Mudanya, the small port on the south shore of the Sea of Marmara which served the city of Bursa now firmly under Turkish control. But Mustafa Kemal would not attend, just as he had earlier refused to meet Harington on board a British warship in the Black Sea, unless his terms were accepted in advance. The Turkish representative would be İsmet Pasha, the Turkish commander of the western front, and Mustafa Kemal's trusted lieutenant. Isolated politically at home and abroad, Lloyd George and Churchill gave way to the peace lobby, albeit with bad grace. Harington, who had earlier disobeyed instructions to confront the Turkish nationalists with an ultimatum, was instructed to be tough in the negotiations. He did not need advice from London to map out common ground for a satisfactory settlement.

The conference began on 3 October in a merchant's house on the waterfront, which had been used by the honorary Russian consul before the war. It was essentially a military meeting between equals: the British, French, Italian and Greek commanders in Istanbul on one side, and İsmet, the Turkish commander on the other. What was under discussion was the gradual transfer of Istanbul and of eastern Thrace to Turkish control. It was not an easy matter to arrange. The capital and its hinterland had a mixed population. Inter-communal relations had broken down, and the prospect of losing Allied protection terrified Christian communities, which had been led to believe that they would replace the Turks as rulers of the cosmopolitan heart of the Ottoman state. There were some 150,000 foreign nationals, most of them natives, who clung to their privileged status. As soon as they entered the Great War, the Young Turks had abrogated the capitulations, under which foreigners came under the jurisdiction of their own consular authorities. The Treaty of Sèvres had restored their extra-territorial status. It was no secret that the Ankara government was determined to abolish this privilege. Suspicions and fears were rife on all sides.

In the circumstances, the delegates could congratulate themselves on coming to an agreement after a week of tough bargaining. The terms signed on 11 October were simple. The Greeks were to evacuate their troops from eastern Thrace within 30 days, transferring civil authority to the Allies, who would also interpose themselves between Greeks and Turks on the frontier. The Allies would in turn hand over the administration to Turkish officials who would be assisted by up to 8,000 Turkish gendarmes. Allied troops would remain in their present positions, i.e. would continue to occupy Istanbul and the Straits, until peace was signed.

The Greek delegate, General Mazarakis, saved face by absenting himself from the signing ceremony. But three days later, on 14 October, the Greek government announced that it would abide by the terms of the armistice. It had no other option. Fighting had ended in effect a month earlier when the last Greek soldier left Anatolia. Now, nearly four years after the defeat of the Ottoman state, and eight years after it had entered the First World War on the side of Germany, hostilities ceased officially. The armistice of Mudros, imposed on the defeated multi-national Ottoman Empire in November 1918, was replaced by an armistice negotiated with the victorious new Turkish national government. Mudros had not ended the fighting; Mudanya did so.

Within a month, all the Greeks – soldiers from the mainland and local civilians – had left eastern Thrace. Villagers loaded their belongings on carriages and carts and drove their cattle with them to the western bank of the Meriç (Maritza/Evros) river. The towns, including the frontier city of Edirne (Adrianople), took years to recover the loss of most of their skilled citizens. In Istanbul, Greeks who wanted to leave had longer to make their arrangements. Within a year some 150,000 had left, including the wealthiest members of the community.[36] In 1914 there had been between two and 2.5 million Greek Orthodox residents in Turkey.[37] By 1927, when the first official census was held in the Turkish Republic, the Greek community was reduced to 150,000, all of them in Istanbul.[38] Today there are fewer than 5,000 Greeks in Turkey.

Eight days after the signing of the armistice at Mudanya, Lloyd George's coalition of Liberals and Conservatives fell apart. Meeting at the Carlton Club on 19 October the Conservatives decided to pull out of the government and fight the forthcoming general elections as an independent party. Lloyd George resigned the following day and was replaced by the Conservative leader Bonar Law. Curzon deserted Lloyd George, whose interference in the conduct of foreign policy he had long resented, and stayed in charge of the Foreign Office. He kept his office when Bonar Law won the general elections on 15 November. Lloyd George, unrepentant to the end, never saw office again. Churchill, who stood by him, put the leisure he had not sought to good use by writing his account of the war and much else besides, until his finest hour came in 1940.

In Greece accounts were settled in a more savage way. The junta court-martialled the country's defeated leaders. After a travesty of a trial, six of them, including the Prime Minister Dimitrios Gounaris and the Commander-in-Chief General Hatzianestis, were sentenced to death on 28 November and shot without further ado. Prince Andrew escaped a similar fate thanks to British intervention. His sentence of exile was a lucky deliverance. Venizelos returned to the international scene, and became Greek representative at the peace conference in Lausanne.

As his foreign enemies bit the dust, Mustafa Kemal was courting, or, more accurately, responding to the advances of a Paris-educated, good-looking, strong-willed young Turkish woman called Lâtife. She was the daughter of a carpet merchant, one of the few successful Turkish businessmen in İzmir, and she set her sights on Mustafa Kemal when he accepted her father's invitation to lodge at his seaside villa in what was at the time a suburb of the city. They were married on 29 January 1923, after Mustafa Kemal's mother, Zübeyde, who opposed the match, had died – also in İzmir. The marriage, which tried unsuccessfully to blend old habits and new expectations, lasted for a thousand tempestuous days, and ended in a Muslim divorce. A few months later, Western-style marriage laws were introduced as part of Mustafa Kemal's reforms, and husbands could no longer demand a divorce as of right.

5

At One with Civilisation

The Turks had been at war, almost without a break, since 1911, the year the Italians invaded Libya. The First World War and the War of Independence, which followed, lasted eight years. But after the Turkish victory at the end of August 1922, the pace quickened. A fortnight later, the Greek army was out of Anatolia. A month after that an armistice was signed with the Allies. It then took another two weeks to sweep away the Ottoman monarchy, which had ruled the country for seven centuries.

On 19 October 1922, a week after the signature of the armistice at Mudanya, General Re'fet (Bele), one of Mustafa Kemal's original companions in the War of Independence, arrived in Istanbul at the head of the force of Turkish gendarmes (in fact, soldiers in gendarmerie uniforms) which was to take over eastern Thrace. Turks in the Ottoman capital received him enthusiastically. The Ankara government had long had a representative in Istanbul with whom Allied High Commissioners dealt. But with Re'fet Pasha's arrival the relationship changed, as power in the old capital slipped out of the hands of the Allied authorities. Welcomed by the Sultan's

ADC and the Grand Vizier, Re'fet made it clear that he recognised Vahdettin as Caliph only and not as temporal sovereign, and his government not at all. Mustafa Kemal had already decided to abolish the monarchy, even though the matter had not been debated in the National Assembly. Re'fet waited ten days before visiting Vahdettin in Yıldız Palace. The Sultan left this account of the audience: 'This little man hid his true intention behind grand aspirations, and said that if I accepted a meaningless caliphate shorn of the constitutional sultanate, which we had all sworn to uphold, and if I sent a telegram to Ankara declaring that I recognised the law of fundamental organisation [the provisional constitution voted by the National Assembly in 1921] and the Ankara government, I could save my person and position. I replied that I had to think it over. But the following day when I read Mustafa Kemal's insults against my person and our dynasty, the time came for a decision.' Re'fet was reported to have said later: 'I crossed my legs in front of the Sultan and leaned back so far that the tip of my shoes nearly touched his nose'.[1] According to the Grand Vizier, Tevfik Pasha, Re'fet told the Sultan: 'Close the palace gates and don't allow anyone in. Unsuitable people are coming and going, and this leads to gossip. You can go to the mosque and nowhere else.' Nevertheless the Sultan received in audience two trusted advisers who were hated in Ankara – Mustafa Sabri, a clerical politician who had served Damad Ferid as Sheikh al-Islam, and the journalist, Ali Kemal, who had infuriated the nationalists by his fiery articles denouncing the resistance movement in Anatolia.[2]

It was not the Sultan, but the Allies who forced a decision. On 27 October, the Principal Allies – Britain, France and Italy – invited both the Istanbul government of Grand Vizier Tevfik Pasha and Mustafa Kemal's Ankara government to send delegations to a peace conference to be held at Lausanne in Switzerland. In response, Tevfik Pasha suggested to Mustafa Kemal that they should discuss the matter, but Kemal would have none of it. There was only one Turkish government, he insisted, the Ankara government formed by the National Assembly. He did not need the help or advice of Tevfik Pasha and his ministers. The Sultan's government was defunct and the time had come for him and his ministers to leave the stage.

On 30 October, Dr Rıza Nur, a maverick politician who had opposed the CUP before joining Mustafa Kemal in Ankara (and who was later to break with him and vilify him in his memoirs), tabled a bill in the Assembly, declaring that the Sultan's government had ceased to exist when the Allies forcibly closed down the Ottoman parliament on 16 March 1920. From that date, sovereignty, which had been appropriated by the Ottoman dynasty, had reverted to the Turkish nation. The Sultanate was now abolished, but the dynasty would continue to exercise the function of Caliphate at the discretion of the National Assembly. It was in Mustafa Kemal's mind a transitional arrangement, but he argued for it eloquently, saying: *On the one hand, the people of Turkey will become daily stronger as a modern and civilised state, and realise increasingly their humanity ... and, on the other, the institution of the Caliphate will be exalted as the central link of the spirit, the conscience and the faith of the Islamic world.*[3] Modernity and civilisation were synonymous.

Mustafa Kemal reminded his audience that there had been shadowy Caliphs between the 10th and the 16th century when temporal government was exercised by Sultans in the Islamic world. The two functions could, therefore, be separated. But the change of rhetoric was abrupt. When the Assembly opened in Ankara on 23 April 1920, it had pledged loyalty to the Sultan and Caliph. Now it denounced the monarchy and praised a shadowy Caliphate. Inevitably, there was uneasiness in the ranks of the deputies. Could the wording of the bill perhaps be changed? Mustafa Kemal ended the argument the following day, when the matter came up in committee. In his speech in 1927, in which he gave his account of the genesis of the Turkish republic, Mustafa Kemal said that he stood on a bench in the committee room and told members: *Sovereignty and kingship are never decided by academic debate. They are seized by force ... Now the Turkish nation has effectively gained possession of its sovereignty ... This is an accomplished fact ... If those assembled here see the matter in its natural light, we shall all agree. Otherwise, facts will prevail, but some heads may roll.* Thereupon, a member said, 'Sorry, we had approached the matter from a different angle. Now you have set us right.'[4] On 1 November, the full Assembly passed the law abolishing the monarchy. There was only one dissenting vote.

The minutes of the committee have never been published, but whatever the exact words used by Mustafa Kemal, there was no doubt about his intentions. The Grand Vizier took the hint. On 4 November Tevfik Pasha submitted his resignation to the Sultan. Moving into his office, Re'fet informed the Allies that the administration of Istanbul was now in the hands of the Ankara government.

The first consequence was far from reassuring. The nationalists' hate figure, the journalist Ali Kemal (whose great-grandson Boris Johnson, also a journalist and polemicist, was to be elected Mayor of London 85 years later) had tried to make amends by admitting that he had been wrong and the nationalists right. He had believed that salvation lay in cooperation with the Allies. The nationalists had proved that opposition to them was the right course. The tactics differed, but the objective was the same. The admission did not save him. He was kidnapped by nationalist agents in broad daylight in the European heart of Istanbul and taken to İzmit, where 'bearded' Nurettin now had his headquarters. After abusing him as a traitor, Nurettin handed Ali Kemal over to a lynch mob, which beat him to death. Mustafa Kemal made no secret of his disgust at the fate meted out to his opponent.[5] Soon afterwards Nurettin fell into disgrace. He came out as a political opponent of Mustafa Kemal, who denounced him at length in his 1927 speech, and belittled his military career. Henceforth, repression was left to the courts.

News of Ali Kemal's murder terrified Turks who had cooperated with the Allies in Istanbul, and they hastened to seek refuge in the embassies and consulates of Allied states. The following year the peace treaty provided for a general amnesty for political offences. At the same time, the Turkish government undertook to draw up a list of no more than 150 political opponents who were to be exiled from the country. Prominent critics of the nationalist cause could thus make their way to safety abroad. Survivors among them were allowed back into the country in 1938. This act of reconciliation was one of Mustafa Kemal's last political decisions. He died later that year.

Fear of the new regime was keenest in the Sultan's palace at Yıldız. The 'philosopher' Rıza Tevfik, one of the Ottoman signatories of the Sèvres Treaty, reports in his memoirs that rumours had reached the palace that 'Mustafa Kemal Pasha will come to depose the Sultan and have him executed. After all, this Turkish revolution is a replica of the great French Revolution. What the French did to Louis XVI, the Turks will do to Vahdettin. Revolutionaries have no other way.'[6]

The women and servants in the Sultan's private apartments were panic-stricken. 'Come what may, ensure the escape of our lord and master,' they pleaded. But the Sultan had one more matter to settle.

It was a tradition that when the throne was vacated, every single person in the retinue of the late sovereign had to leave the palace. Women in the harem were either married off or entrusted to the care of their relatives. Only elderly servant women who knew the palace ceremonial were allowed to stay on. There had been 36 women in the harem of Vahdettin's brother and predecessor, Sultan Mehmed V (Mehmed Reşad). Vahdettin did not have a harem of his own before his accession, and he allowed 12 women of his brother's harem to stay on. One of them was a young girl, called Nevzad, who celebrated her 19th birthday on 1 November 1922. Vahdettin married her before leaving the country. She was his third wife: the first had borne him two daughters, and the second his only son and heir, Mehmed Ertuğrul, who was ten years old in 1922, and was to die in Cairo in 1944. All three women joined Vahdettin in exile in Italy.

Vahdettin had always been fearful for his safety. Even before his accession to the throne he carried a handgun in his pocket, and he continued to do so to the end of his life. His audience was surprised one day when the gun fell noisily to the floor. Indecisive in most matters, he was, it seems, a good shot. But now safety had to be sought by other means. On 16 November Vahdettin wrote this letter to the Allied Commander-in-Chief General Harington: 'I consider my life to be in danger in Istanbul, and I therefore take refuge with the noble British state and ask for transport from Istanbul to some other destination.'[7] He signed it Mehmed Vahdettin, Caliph of the Muslims, and not Sultan. Forewarned, Harington had already been authorised to make the necessary arrangements. The following day at dawn an ambulance drew up at the gate of Yıldız palace. Vahdettin was smuggled on board. There was a delay on the way to the harbour as a tyre had to be changed. Eventually, Vahdettin, his son, and a suite of ten courtiers arrived at the quayside. It was raining heavily.

Harington was waiting to see off the last Ottoman Sultan. Vahdettin took out a gold cigarette case and lit a cigarette with trembling hands. Harington is said to have expected to be given the cigarette case as a souvenir. But retentive to the last, Vahdettin put it back in his pocket, as he asked Harington to make sure that his wives joined him abroad. He then embarked on the British battleship HMS *Malaya* which was standing by in the harbour. Asked whether he would be happy to be taken to Malta, Vahdettin agreed. From Malta he made his way to Mecca, ruled precariously by the British protégé King Hussein, who had led a rebellion against the Ottoman state. Mecca, which was about to fall to Ibn Saud, did not provide an agreeable environment, and Vahdettin went on to take up residence in a villa at San Remo on the Italian Riviera. He died there in 1926. His young wife Nevzad was at his bedside. It is said that the local Italian court took the unusual step of sequestering Vahdettin's coffin in an attempt to secure payments of his debts. Somehow a settlement was reached with his creditors, and the coffin was shipped to Damascus where Vahdettin was finally buried.[8] HMS *Malaya* was to make a return visit to Istanbul in 1938. On board was the British guard of honour which took part in Mustafa Kemal's funeral procession.

Superstitious observers noted that Vahdettin had brought ill fortune on himself. He suffered from rheumatism and walked with difficulty. When he entered the old palace at

Topkapı for his accession ceremony in 1918, he had asked for his ebony walking stick. Told that it had been left behind, he exclaimed 'What a disaster!' This word of ill omen, uttered at the beginning of the reign, was bound to bring bad luck in the end. The ebony walking stick was the last object Vahdettin took with him when he left his palace for ever.[9]

As soon as he left the country, Vahdettin issued a statement declaring 'I have not fled. I have migrated'.[10] It was a reference to the Prophet Muhammad whose move from Mecca to Medina in AD 622, known as the *hijra*, is the beginning of the Muslim era. Vahdettin insisted that he had not abdicated and that the Ottoman throne was still his by right. He pleaded in vain. On 18 November, the day after his escape, the chief cleric who acted as a minister of the Ankara government issued a *fatwa* ruling that it was lawful to depose the fugitive Sultan. The Assembly immediately implemented the decision. It then proceeded to elect Vahdettin's cousin Abdülmecid, the heir apparent, to the newly defined position of Caliph.

Vahdettin had tried to rule as well as reign, like his eldest brother Abdülhamid II and unlike his other brother and predecessor Mehmed V. He claimed that he followed Abdülhamid's policy when he sought the friendship of Britain and France. Abdülhamid had in fact relied on Germany to offset Britain's political and France's economic power, and he used his title of Caliph to frighten European empires, worried about the loyalty of their Muslim subjects. The power equation had changed with the defeat of Germany and the triumph of Bolshevism in Russia. Britain and, to a lesser extent, France had a choice of Muslim puppets, and certainly by 1922 they had come to the conclusion that they could do without Vahdettin, either as Sultan or as nominal Caliph of all Muslims. True, the Ottoman Caliphate had supporters in India, but it was the survival of Turkey as an independent Muslim country rather than of the Ottoman dynasty that was the aim of the *Khilafat* movement in the sub-continent. That is why it sent money to the Turkish resistance movement, led by Mustafa Kemal, and opposed Lloyd George's design to partition the most important surviving independent Muslim country. After the First World War, decolonisation rather than Pan-Islamism became the dominant ideology of elites among the Muslim subjects of European empires. Nostalgia was the only resource left to the Ottoman dynasty.

The shift in the ideological climate was beyond Vahdettin's grasp. He had trained himself in traditional Islamic culture during his long years of seclusion before his accession to the throne in 1918. The CUP had been modernist. Vahdettin turned away from the modern world. Abdülhamid II was interested in photography and had a photographic studio in his palace in Yıldız. Vahdettin's interest lay in Islamic calligraphy, classical Ottoman poetry and music. In all three he had ability, but not an outstanding talent. Abdülmecid, his successor as last Caliph, preferred Western arts. He composed Western palm-court music, and was a competent portrait painter. Disregarding Islamic objections to the representation of the human form, he chose for his paintings subjects such as 'Beethoven in the Harem' and 'Goethe in the Harem', as well as 'Palace Concubine'. His interests did not endear him either to the elite or to the people. He practised Western arts, but thought of himself as a champion of Asia against Europe. One of his last political gestures in exile in German-occupied Paris was to send a telegram to the Japanese Emperor congratulating him on the success of his forces after Pearl Harbor.[11] Bad judgement was characteristic of the last days of the Ottoman dynasty.

In spite of his tactical praise for the institution of a spiritual Caliphate, Mustafa Kemal was beginning to show his real feelings towards religion. On 2 October 1922, when he made his triumphal entry into Ankara to announce the victory of his armies, he was met at the door of the National Assembly by a uniformed imam, who started reciting a prayer of thanksgiving in Arabic. Mustafa Kemal pushed him aside. *There is no need for this here*, he said. *You can say your prayers in a mosque. We have won the war not with prayers, but with the blood of our soldiers.*[12] He had mobilised Muslim religious sentiment at home and abroad to fight foreign invaders. He decided he could dispense with it now. But, at this stage, he took care not to confront Islam as such. In an off-the-record briefing he gave to leading Istanbul journalists in January 1923, he asked them not to describe the government as irreligious. That would be tantamount to an invitation to the public to attack him. The people, he explained, were not without a religion. They professed the Muslim faith. *No one is rejecting religion, the way the Communists do*, he said. Anyway, Communism was nonsense, and when Russia abandoned it, it would become stronger than it had been under the Tsars.[13] When a journalist asked whether the government itself would be religious, he was vague. *Will it or won't it? I don't know. There is nothing in the laws today to prevent it.* However, he indicated his own position when he added: *If you insist, call the government materialist, but not irreligious.*[14] He made no bones about his dislike of Muslim clerics, the *hocas* (hodjas). They were, he said, a worthless lot. The *medreses* (religious schools), where they taught, had been a resort of draft-dodgers during the War of Independence.[15] Talking to tradesmen in the southern city of Adana later that year, he made the claim that has dominated secularist discourse in Turkey to this day. *The evils which have ruined and enslaved our nation have all been wrought in the name of religion*, he said. There was no need to consult religious scholars (*ulema*). *Whatever is rational, whatever is in the interest of the nation and of the Muslim community, is also in conformity with religion. For if our religion had not been rational, it would not have been the perfect and the final religion.*[16]

Mustafa Kemal had earlier addressed the faithful from the pulpit of a mosque in Balıkesir in western Anatolia. Preachers, he said, should use a language everyone understood, in other words, Turkish not Arabic. They should follow developments in science, politics, society and civilisation, and their sermons should be in conformity with scientific truths.[17] Then, step by step, religion was banished from the public sphere altogether. Truth was to be found solely in contemporary scientific civilisation. If Islam equalled rationalism, then rationalism was sufficient.

However, the full secularisation of the state could wait a little longer. The immediate job after the conclusion of the armistice was to prepare for the peace conference in Lausanne. Mustafa Kemal was pleased with the way İsmet had brought the armistice negotiations at Mudanya to a successful conclusion, and decided to appoint him chief Turkish delegate in the final peace talks. True, İsmet was a soldier, not a diplomat. At Mudanya he had acted within his competence, as he faced Allied military commanders. At Lausanne he would have to argue with foreign ministers. İsmet himself was nervous about his qualifications. Mustafa Kemal brushed aside his reservations. İsmet was loyal and he fully shared his leader's vision. That was enough.

As the Lausanne conference was held at foreign minister level, the first step was to appoint İsmet Foreign Minister, and then to choose his delegation. He was given two assistant delegates (one of them the sharp-tongued Rıza Nur) and 25 advisers. Some were members of the Assembly, others career civil servants who had served the Ottoman government. Inevitably, the new civil service was recruited largely from among members of the Ottoman bureaucracy. One of the advisers was the former Unionist minister, Cavid Bey, an acknowledged expert in financial affairs. There was also one eccentric but astute choice – the chief rabbi Hayim Nahum. Unlike the Christians, the Jewish community had remained loyal to the Ottoman state, and Hayim Nahum could be relied upon to make use of his foreign contacts to advance the interests of the new government in Ankara. That he was a critic of Zionism was an additional advantage. It meant that his loyalty was not divided. Nahum was described as a teacher of French, the official language of the conference.

When İsmet arrived in Lausanne, he was told that the opening would be postponed for a few days to await the results of the British general elections. Was this a British trick? he wondered. The French hastened to reassure him. Prime Minister Poincaré invited him to Paris where he told İsmet that peace would definitely be concluded.[18] In Britain, the Conservatives won the election on 15 November. Curzon, happy to be rid of the constant interference of Lloyd George, stayed on as Foreign Secretary under the new Prime Minister, Bonar Law. Before going to Lausanne, he too met Poincaré and the newly installed Italian dictator Benito Mussolini. But the united Allied front which Curzon wanted to form against Turks was shaky.

The conference was opened on 20 November by the Swiss President Robert Haab in the Mont Benon casino. İsmet thought that after the inaugural speech the meeting would break up until the first working session the following morning. But when Curzon insisted on speaking on behalf of the Allies, İsmet gave an impromptu reply in his schoolboy French (as he said himself). The peace conference was to be held between equals, not between a coalition of victors and a vanquished country. Sir Horace Rumbold, the British High Commissioner in Istanbul who had been summoned to Lausanne as Curzon's assistant, believed that İsmet had a great advantage. 'In the last resort,' he wrote, 'the Turks will not shrink from the use of force, while the mere thought of hostilities is repugnant to Bonar Law's mind.'[19] Rumbold did not realise that Mustafa Kemal was just as averse to the resumption of hostilities. Both sides bluffed. But Mustafa Kemal had a clearer idea of his objective. This was the total independence of Turkey and, therefore, an end to foreign interference in Turkish internal affairs. The premise of the Sèvres Treaty had been that the Turks were incapable of running their own state, whether in the management of the economy or in the administration of justice, or even in public health. Mustafa Kemal was determined that this judgment should be reversed at Lausanne. He was well aware of his country's backwardness, but he was convinced that his people had in them the capacity to run a successful state in the modern world.

The peace conference ranged far and wide. There were 12 national delegations – four host Allied countries (the fourth being Japan, which had little to say), five countries, including Turkey, invited to attend all sessions (one of them, the USA, did not consider itself a party to the proceedings, while pursuing its own interests), the Soviet Union, invited to take part in the discussions of navigation through the Straits, and, for some reason, Belgium and Portugal (but not Spain, which had represented Greek interests in Istanbul in the absence of proper diplomatic relations). The last two were asked to state their views on some topics only.

Curzon was determined to dominate this unwieldy gathering. Poincaré and Mussolini left after the opening, and Curzon declared himself chairman on behalf of the Allied hosts. This might have encouraged the Greeks, reliant as ever on British support, to make impossible demands. But Venizelos, who was the chief Greek delegate, had learnt his lesson. In his heart of hearts he had always believed in disengagement between Greeks and Turks, in what a Turkish observer called *divorce total*. He had been unable to get it on his own terms, but this did not alter the fact that peace between the two peoples could not be secured any other way. Greece had been defeated and was bankrupt. But Turkey too was in dire straits: many of its cities lay in ruins; it was poor and backward. Both countries had a common interest in peace.

Turkey's frontiers with the Soviet Union and French-Mandated Syria had already been fixed by bilateral treaties. For the rest, the usual practice of *uti possidetis* prevailed: the final peace treaty was to legitimise facts on the ground. Eastern Thrace was already in Turkish hands; Mosul was occupied by the British as Mandatory power in Iraq. The National Pact, voted by the last Ottoman parliament, had claimed İskenderun/Alexandretta and the province of Mosul, and demanded referendums to determine the future of western Thrace and of the territory lost to Russia in the Caucasus in 1878. The treaties approved by the National Assembly during the War of Independence had already conceded İskenderun to the French, and Batum (but not the rest of the three districts originally lost to Russia) to the Soviet Union.

Mustafa Kemal was a realist: Turkish claims which were unlikely to succeed could be used as bargaining counters. But his political opponents in the National Assembly played the nationalist card and demanded that the Turkish delegation in Lausanne should insist on the full implementation of the National Pact. The opposition in the Assembly was joined by the Prime Minister Rauf (Orbay), the chief Ottoman signatory of the armistice signed in Mudros in 1918, and subsequently a principled nationalist supporter of Mustafa Kemal. Rauf had hoped to be the chief delegate in Lausanne, and was now determined to make İsmet's life difficult. İsmet played fair by asking the government's permission before departing in any way from the instructions he had been given. But he infuriated Rauf by copying his reports to Mustafa Kemal. He had other readers, unknown to him: the British had broken the code used by the Turkish delegation and were fully aware of his tactics. İsmet realised that there were leaks, but thought that these occurred in Ankara.[20]

Frontiers were not the main issue of contention, as Britain and Turkey agreed to set aside the fate of Mosul for subsequent negotiations and, ultimately, for arbitration by the newly-established League of Nations. Curzon's admirers attributed Turkish concessions to the British foreign secretary's encyclopaedic knowledge which allowed him to argue convincingly that Kurds, who were the majority in the province of Mosul, were ethnically distinct from the Turks. This, however, was hardly news to İsmet. His point was that Turks and Kurds formed a single community, united by common interests. Curzon did not dispose of the argument that sorting out Kurds from Turks would not serve the interests of either people.

The Kurds would rather be ruled by Turks than by Arabs. Their resistance to incorporation in an Arab Iraq was broken by British aerial bombing, accompanied by the promise that the British would stay on until Kurdish rights were secured. This is what happened in theory. In reality, the Kurds of Mosul were better off than their kinsmen in Turkey so long as British influence was paramount in Iraq. The moment that influence ceased, the Arabs tried to impose their rule on the Kurds, who resisted at great cost to themselves. The conflict continues to this day.

While the fate of Mosul was left in suspense at Lausanne, a settlement was agreed on the status of the Turkish Straits. The zone of the Straits was to be demilitarised, and free navigation was to be ensured under the supervision of an international commission. Soviet Russia wanted the Straits to be closed always to warships of countries which did not border on it. It was disappointed and did not sign the text which was eventually agreed. However friendly relations between Moscow and Ankara were preserved, as both governments had other priorities.

After long and laborious negotiations, the political problems between Britain and Turkey were largely overcome. Now it was France, with which Turkey had already signed what amounted to a preliminary peace treaty, which delayed a final peace settlement. France stood out for the interests of its investors in the defunct Ottoman state. It believed that these could be safeguarded only if foreigners retained their extra-territorial privileges under the regime of capitulations. This meant setting a limit to Turkish sovereign independence. İsmet stood out for his country's untrammelled sovereignty. Special facilities could be granted to foreigners (and to non-Muslim communities in Turkey) only if they were reciprocated. Similarly, any settlement of economic claims should not impose impossible burdens on Turkey.

Mustafa Kemal probably overestimated the power of

CONTROL OF THE TURKISH STRAITS

The Straits consist of two narrow sea passages separating Europe from Asia – the Bosphorus in the north, and the Dardanelles in the south, with the Sea of Marmara (usually spelled Marmora in Ottoman times) in between. During the First World War the Western Allies found that Turkish control of the Straits stopped them from supplying Russia. They, therefore, sought in the treaties of Sèvres and then of Lausanne to ensure that Turkey should not obstruct free passage. This is why they insisted that Turkish troops should be kept out of the area. When, however, the post-war settlement was challenged first by Italy and then by Germany, it was these countries, rather than Turkey, that were seen as a threat to free navigation. Turkey's natural wish to regain the capacity to defend the Straits, with the great city of Istanbul extending over both shores of the Bosphorus, found a favourable response in the West. This led to the signing in 1936 of the Convention of Montreux, which replaced the agreement on the status of the Straits appended to the Treaty of Lausanne. The Montreux Convention, allowing Turkey to re-militarise the Straits, and making it responsible for regulating traffic through it, laid down detailed rules for navigation. It provided for free passage for commercial shipping in peacetime, and treated states bordering the Black Sea differently from those which did not. The former could sail their warships freely in peacetime (subject to notice and to the condition that submarines should surface during transit), while the warships of the latter could not stay longer than 21 days in the Black Sea and were subject to tonnage limitations. The provisions did not satisfy the Soviets, who claimed that Axis warships were allowed through as merchant ships during the Second World War. In 1945, therefore, the Soviet Union asked for a revision of the Montreux Convention which would give it a share in the defence of the Straits – in other words, the right to a military presence in the area. Thanks to US support, Turkey was able to resist this demand. Later, the Americans were keen to demonstrate their right to send warships into the Black Sea and resented Turkish insistence on the limitations on tonnage and length of stay stipulated in the Convention. They also disputed the Soviet description of aircraft carriers (which are subject to separate restrictions) as cruisers. Turkey too found the provision on unrestricted commercial navigation irksome as it sought to regulate the passage through the Bosphorus of supertankers, whose cargoes of oil threatened the safety of the greatly expanded Istanbul metropolitan area. In view of the difficulty of renegotiating the Convention, the countries concerned have learnt to live with its provisions, which Turkey continues to implement meticulously.

Britain, a country which he certainly admired, even though it had been his principal opponent. Like other Turks, educated in the Western mould, he had a better understanding of the French, and this helped him to drive a wedge between the two Principal Allies. Curzon, bruised in earlier encounters with the French, tried his best to preserve a common Allied front. When İsmet refused to budge on capitulations, the settlement of Ottoman debt and compensation claims – where the French were particularly demanding – Curzon tried to twist his arm by appeals to self-interest. İsmet liked to tell the story that Curzon countered his insistence on Turkey's unconditional independence by saying: 'We are not happy … We've been unable to have our way on any point. But all the proposals you have rejected are still in our pockets. You're taking over a ruined country. You'll certainly need money to build it up. You'll come and kneel before us to get that money. That's when I'll present to you one by one all the demands you're now rejecting.'[21] Curzon may well have thought so, but he is unlikely to have been so crude. Whatever his exact words, İnönü's account enjoys universal credence in Turkey, and is frequently quoted by nationalists today as they denounce sales of Turkish assets to foreigners and the evils of globalisation.

Unable to make headway in the face of İsmet's stubborn resistance, Curzon issued what amounted to an ultimatum. On 30 January 1923, he asked İsmet to sign a text which, he argued, represented the final Allied position. But Curzon's stand was undermined by Poincaré who told the press that the treaty, as it stood, formed only 'a basis for discussion' and no more. This made it easier for İsmet to refuse to sign. It was a dramatic moment. The British delegation had packed its bags, but the train which was to take them away was delayed in case İsmet changed his mind. He did not. There was no alternative to breaking off negotiations and adjourning the conference.

Curzon's superior airs were widely mocked behind his back. His discomfiture when his drunken valet stole all his trousers and hid them under his bed to cover up his hoard of empty bottles made the rounds of clubs in London. His assistant, Sir Horace Rumbold, was Blimpish beyond parody. He thought that 'an uppish oriental' was 'an unpleasant animal', and was proud of the fact that he had never asked a Turk inside his house when he was High Commissioner in Istanbul. But his prejudices, which were shared by his colleagues, did not always impair his judgment. As the Lausanne conference ground to a halt, he predicted in a private letter that the Turks would not sign the treaty. He added that the French also were discontented with it, believing that it gave Britain what it wanted, but did not give France the economic benefits for which it had hoped.[22] He was right, but he disregarded one other factor.

The Americans, who did not take part in the negotiations, nevertheless watched them carefully to make sure that the open-door principle giving all states equal access to international markets was respected, except where their own interests would be served by privileged treatment. They were particularly interested in a project originally formulated before the First World War by the retired US admiral Colby Chester. In its revived form, the Chester Concession provided for the construction by an American company of railways and harbours on a vast scale in eastern Turkey in exchange for the exclusive right to exploit mineral resources lying within 20 kilometres on either side of the new railways. The Kirkuk oilfield in the province of Mosul was the prize coveted by the Americans. Competition between the Americans and the British, who wanted to retain control of Mosul, suited the Turks in their effort to regain the area, and the National Assembly approved the deal on 9 April 1923. But eight months later it rescinded its decision, after the US had distanced itself from the Near Eastern peace settlement, and it had become clear that it was not going to intervene in the Mosul dispute.

While a mass of unfinished business was left on the table, Greece and Turkey signed two important agreements on 30 January, the day the conference was adjourned. The first met an urgent humanitarian concern by providing for the exchange of prisoners of war and civilian detainees. As a result, thousands of Greek prisoners did not have to wait for the final peace settlement to regain their freedom. The second agreement had more profound long-term implications. It provided for an exchange of populations which covered all Ottoman subjects professing the Greek (Eastern) Orthodox faith in Turkey, and all Muslims in Greece. There were two exceptions: Greeks in Istanbul and on two islands off the entrance to the Dardanelles, Imvros (later renamed Gökçeada) and Tenedhos (Bozcaada), which reverted to Turkey, could stay on, provided they had been resident there when the First World War started. The same provision applied to Muslims in Western Thrace, which Greece had gained from Bulgaria – its only prize for its involvement in the War. The numbers of the two communities were roughly equal at 150–200,000.

The Greek Patriarchate could thus stay on in Istanbul. The Greek Patriarch is accepted by all Eastern Orthodox Christians as Ecumenical (in other words, universal) Patriarch, the most senior prelate in their church. However, as far as the Turks are concerned, the Patriarch is simply the religious leader of the Greek Orthodox community in the country. It was therefore agreed in Lausanne that he should be a Turkish citizen. This remains the official position of the Turkish government to this day. İsmet wanted the exchange of populations to be total, with no exceptions for Istanbul and Western Thrace. This would have prevented much trouble in years to come. However, there was value also in preserving this most important link with the city's imperial (and, therefore, multiethnic) past. Life might have been simpler, but Istanbul would have been poorer without it. It was a reminder of the destiny of Istanbul as a world city. The preservation of some traces of its cosmopolitan past held the promise of a cosmopolitan future built on new foundations.

For the rest, most Greeks had already left Turkey, fleeing with the Greek army. But there were two Greek communities which had been cut off. Many of the Greeks who lived along the coast of the Black Sea had been deported to the interior, and for them resettlement in Greece came as a liberation. The other isolated community was made up of the Turkish-speaking Greeks of central Anatolia, an area known as Karaman (Caramania in Western literature) before the rise of the Ottoman state. These Caramanian Greeks (*Karamanlı* in Turkish; *Karamanlidhes* in Greek) found it difficult to adapt to life in Greece, where they were mocked as Christians 'baptized in yoghurt'. They retaliated by referring to natives of Greece as 'Vlachs' – Romanian-speaking shepherds. Initial difficulties fostered survival techniques, and the descendants of the *Karamanlidhes* gradually rose to prominence in their new homeland.

As for the Muslims who had lived in Greece during the centuries of Ottoman rule, many had migrated to Turkey before 1914, when independent Greece emerged in 1830 and then acquired Ottoman Thessaly in 1878, and most of Ottoman Macedonia in 1913. The exchange of populations of 1923 completed the process, except in western Thrace and for the small Turkish community in the Dodecanese islands, ruled by the Italians from 1911 to 1945.

The break in the conference on 30 January 1923 was not an unmitigated disaster for the participants. But there were dangers too. Rumbold, who returned to his post as High Commissioner in Istanbul, had to deal with fears that the Turks might seize the city by force. One contingency plan provided for the withdrawal of British troops from Istanbul to a fortified enclave in Gallipoli. In the fevered atmosphere of Istanbul, with its large population of panicky local Christians, British authorities found it hard to realise that Mustafa Kemal was a careful and patient statesman, averse to military adventures,

İsmet had his own difficulties, as critics in the Assembly blamed him for making unnecessary concessions, which had not in the event saved the conference. Mustafa Kemal responded by touring the country to mobilise popular support. He returned to Ankara after he had outlined his reconstruction policy at the economic congress in İzmir, and made sure that the Assembly approved reasonable counter-proposals for the resumption of the Peace Conference.

As soon as the Allies agreed to send their delegates back to Lausanne, Mustafa Kemal prevailed on the Assembly to dissolve itself and fix a date for new elections. He then drew up a party manifesto and vetted all the candidates his embryonic party was to put forward. However, Rauf was still Prime Minister when the peace conference resumed in Lausanne on 23 April, exactly three years after the opening of the Turkish National Assembly in Ankara. Curzon who had already secured all the main British interests, did not return to Lausanne, and left Rumbold in charge. İsmet went back to face French insistence on special treatment for its economic and cultural interests. The capitulations were again the most troublesome problem. Adamant that they should be abolished, İsmet advanced to his objective step by step. In his reminiscences he gives this account of his discussions with the French legal expert, Henri Fromageot.

'His draft opened with the words "To prepare the ground for the reform and abolition of the capitulations ...". "No need," I said, "of preparing the ground ... Why not say simply 'the capitulations are abolished?'" "You can't," he replied, "you must use legal language." Well, I didn't master their legal language in nine months. Then one day Fromageot came to me with the same article. "What do you want?" he asked. "Write 'the capitulations have been abolished, finished and done with'" I replied. "All right," he said. "Have it your way." "What's happened to your legal language?" I asked. "They have come to a decision to do away with the capitulations," he replied. "So they hadn't decided earlier." "No they hadn't."'[23]

One by one the other difficulties were disposed of. The French agreed that their bondholders should be repaid in francs at the current rate of exchange, and not in gold, as they insisted earlier. The Ottoman public debt was apportioned among all the successor states. Letters were exchanged on conditions governing foreign schools, concessions granted earlier to foreigners, and so on. Now and then, İsmet made some temporary concessions: he agreed that Turkey would not increase its customs duties for five years, and that, also for five years, it would employ a few foreign advisers in the administration of justice and public health. Only one difficulty remained. It was clear to İsmet that there was no point in pressing Greece for reparations. The Greeks could not pay anyway. He offered to waive Turkish claims in exchange for a frontier rectification by which Turkey would gain Karaağaç, a suburb of Edirne (Adrianople), and the site of the city's railway station, which lay on the western (Greek) bank of the Meriç (Maritza/Evros) river. But back in Ankara, Rauf would not hear of it. Exasperated, İsmet threatened to break off negotiations and return to Ankara if the concessions he had made were not endorsed.

Mustafa Kemal, to whom he copied the telegram, knew that this was a subject open to demagogic exploitation. Rauf could say 'We cannot give up our claim of reparations against the Greeks who have wrecked our country. Not after our great victory.' He proceeded carefully to save Rauf's face, while İsmet waited impatiently for permission to sign the peace treaty. Finally, on 19 July, Mustafa Kemal cabled to İsmet: *I congratulate you most warmly on your success and await confirmation that the treaty has been signed.*[24] Rauf did not associate himself with the congratulations. Nor did he meet İsmet when he returned to Ankara after the signing of the peace settlement. He resigned on 4 August. A week later, the newly-elected Assembly held its first session and Mustafa Kemal's friend, Fethi (Okyar) became the new Prime Minister.

The Treaty of Lausanne was signed on 24 July 1923. It was an extraordinarily detailed document, running to 143 articles with 20 appendices and associated covenants. Agreement had not been easy, as Mustafa Kemal had realised from the start. *The problems discussed round the peace table at Lausanne had not arisen during the last three or four years*, he said. *Centuries-old scores had to be settled.*[25] But in the end the work was done solidly. Of all the treaties concluded after the Great War, the Lausanne Treaty alone has survived. The Turkish insistence that it should be a treaty freely negotiated by all the parties has paid off. Even Greece, whose defeat it sealed, accepted it as the permanent basis for its relations with its neighbour, Turkey.

The Treaty of Lausanne was inspired by a principle which seemed self-evident until recent times. When the guns fell silent, and no state was willing or able to alter the outcome, then a treaty which recognised it was concluded between the warring parties. The practice was generally observed until after the Second World War. Since then, the outcomes of many local conflicts still await official recognition. The United Nations is unwilling or unable either to change or to recognise by formal treaty new facts on the ground in Palestine, Kashmir, Cyprus, Western Sahara or, more recently, former Yugoslavia and the Caucasus. The absence of treaties bringing closure to conflicts fosters intransigence on all sides and stops refugees from making new lives for themselves. Greek, Turkish and other refugees from the wars of Ottoman succession were quickly resettled. Some benefited from foreign aid; others did not. All had to make the best of their new circumstances.

'The problems discussed round the peace table at Lausanne had not arisen during the last three or four years. Centuries-old scores had to be settled.'
MUSTAFA KEMAL

However, there were two absent parties at Lausanne, and these continue to nurse grievances against the Near Eastern peace settlement. The first was Armenia, a signatory to the unratified Sèvres Treaty. The Lausanne Treaty made no mention of Armenia, whose frontier with Turkey was decided by the 1921 Treaty of Kars. When the small, truncated Armenia regained its independence after the dissolution of the Soviet Union, it refused to explicitly recognise the treaty signed by its predecessor, the Soviet Socialist Republic of Armenia. This may be remedied soon.

Kurdish nationalism poses the more serious threat to the Lausanne settlement. The Treaty of Sèvres provided for an independent Kurdistan, to be carved out of Turkey, should the Kurds want it and prove capable of sustaining it. Turkish Kurdistan could then link up with the Kurdish areas of the province of Mosul. The Treaty of Lausanne does not mention Kurds. But their cultural rights are covered obliquely by Article 39. This provides that 'no restrictions shall be imposed on the free use by any Turkish national of any language in private intercourse, in commerce, religion, in the press, or in publications of any kind or at public meetings. Notwithstanding the existence of the official language, adequate facilities shall be given to Turkish nationals of non-Turkish speech for the oral use of their own language before the Courts.'[26] This provision awaits implementation to this day. Restrictions placed on the use of the Kurdish language (or rather languages) in Turkey are resented by all Turkish citizens of Kurdish origin. Nationalists among them want more, their demands ranging from autonomy to full independence.

Mustafa Kemal was well aware that Kurdish nationalism could tear apart the living tissue of Muslim society in Anatolia. In an off-the-record briefing to Turkish journalists a few months before the Lausanne Treaty was signed, he said: *Mosul is very important for us. First, its environs contain oil-fields which are a source of immense wealth. Secondly, there is the problem of Kurdishness, which is no less important. The English want to form a Kurdish government there. If they do so, the idea might spread to Kurds on our side of the border. To prevent this, the frontier should be drawn further south. But, at the same time, are we to carry on fighting if we don't get Mosul? I ask you: now that it's all over, is it reasonable to continue the war for Mosul?*[27] He added that he was expressing his own opinion, and that the final decision rested with the National Assembly.

Nevertheless, Turkey tried hard to regain Mosul by all means short of war. It signed a new agreement with Soviet Russia to put pressure on the British. It sent an officer into Iraqi Kurdistan to raise the Kurds against the British. But in 1926 when, after the failure of direct negotiations, the League of Nations ruled against it, Turkey conceded Mosul to the British-Mandated Kingdom of Iraq.

It can be argued that by then Britain was on the brink of giving up Mosul. But Turkey had its own difficulties, including a Kurdish rising which it attributed wrongly to British instigation. Eighty years later, Iraq is in danger of breaking up following the US-led invasion, and the prospect of an independent or quasi-independent Iraqi Kurdistan is worrying many Turks, including the military who have to bear the brunt of the terrorist campaign waged by Kurdish separatists from bases across the Iraqi frontier.

Would Turkey have been better off if it had regained Mosul in 1923? Its budget would have benefited from the revenue of the Kirkuk oilfields. But it would have had to administer many more Kurds, as well as more Arabs. The Ottoman Empire had practised multiculturalism, but this had hastened its demise. None of the successor states of the Ottoman, Austro-Hungarian and Russian empires in eastern Europe and the Balkans followed the sort of multicultural policies which are recommended today. Mustafa Kemal recognised the problem, but he had other priorities. The modernisation of Turkey came first, and for its sake he opted for good relations with all the Great Powers.

The failure of the Lausanne Treaty to award Mosul to Turkey was the main objection raised by the opposition when the newly-elected Assembly debated ratification on 23 August. But the opposition had been reduced to a handful of deputies, and the treaty was overwhelmingly approved. The immediate need was to end the Allied occupation of Istanbul, which was to follow ratification. On 2 October Allied occupation troops left Istanbul. Four days later Turkish troops entered the city, while the last Allied soldiers left Gallipoli. On 13 October, the Assembly voted to move the capital of the Turkish state from Istanbul to Ankara.

The old Ottoman capital was demoted to the status of a provincial city. Civil servants had to move to Ankara. Trade suffered, as the transit of goods to and from Russia was reduced to a trickle after the Bolshevik revolution. The city was impoverished by the departure of many foreigners and indigenous non-Muslims. The new regime was not popular in Istanbul. Sensing this, Mustafa Kemal kept away from the old capital, which he had last seen in May 1919. It was only in June 1927, after he had consolidated his personal power, that he went back to Istanbul on the first of what became his regular summer trips to the city. By then the first statue to Mustafa Kemal had been erected on Seraglio Point at the entrance to the harbour.

Mustafa Kemal Atatürk in 1935.

III

The Aftermath

6

Creating a New State and Nation

The Treaty of Lausanne is the founding document of the Turkish national state. But the form, character and institutions of that state had yet to be decided when it was concluded. İsmet had signed it as the representative of the awkwardly named Government of the Grand National Assembly of Turkey. Soon the country was to acquire its new name. On 28 October 1923, Mustafa Kemal invited a group of supporters to dinner in his residence at Çankaya, on the outskirts of Ankara and told them without further ado: *Tomorrow we will proclaim the Republic.*[1] The following day a bill to this effect was tabled and approved by the Assembly after a brief discussion. Elected first President of the Republic, Mustafa Kemal appointed İsmet as his Prime Minister, while Fethi moved over to become Speaker of Parliament. The citizens of Istanbul, including the government's representative Re'fet, learnt of the decision only when a 101-gun salute greeted the birth of the Republic on 29 October.

The circle of Mustafa Kemal's companions in the War of Independence gradually fell apart. Rauf was the first to move away when he was overridden over the terms of the

Lausanne treaty. The sudden proclamation of the Republic cost the friendship of all those nationalist commanders who had not been consulted beforehand. They believed that they were joint authors of the victory in '*Our* War of Independence' – the title given to his memoirs by Kâzım Karabekir, the commander who first welcomed Mustafa Kemal in Anatolia and stood by him when he was dismissed by the Sultan. They wanted, therefore, a voice in the shaping and the government of the state, and they demanded this in the name of democracy. As an opposition journalist argued in Istanbul, the proclamation of a republic was not sufficient guarantee of the freedom of citizens. Republics could harbour dictators as in Latin America. Mustafa Kemal responded by hauling opposition journalists before a revolutionary court in Istanbul. They were acquitted, having been warned that criticism would not deflect Mustafa Kemal from the course he had chosen. In 1927 he offered this explanation for the defection of his original supporters: *In the development of the nation's life which has led to today's republic and its laws, some of the travellers who had started together on the road of national struggle began to resist and oppose me as we crossed the limits of what they could comprehend or sympathise with.*[2]

'Some of the travellers who had started together on the road of national struggle began to resist and oppose me as we crossed the limits of what they could comprehend or sympathise with.'
MUSTAFA KEMAL

The radicalism of Mustafa Kemal's project was indeed hard for them to accept. The nationalist commanders who had sided with Mustafa Kemal had no particular love for the monarchy or for established religion. They were not reactionaries or backward-looking, as was claimed against them.

They too admired the achievements of the West. But they were not prepared to sever all links with the past and alter their whole way of life. They were not democrats, but they wanted to have a voice in government. Mustafa Kemal was prepared to listen to other people's opinions. But he insisted that his decision should be final. Provided his will prevailed, he did not interfere with the administration. As a successful military commander, he knew how to choose subordinates capable of carrying out his orders, and how to delegate.

Mustafa Kemal's determination did not exclude prudence. Before proceeding with his cultural revolution in Turkey, he made sure that the army would remain loyal to him. The nation's will was sovereign, and the peasant, he declared, was the true master of the country. But power was in the barrel of a gun. Mustafa Kemal was lucky in that he found a respected professional soldier to whom he could entrust the command of the armed forces. Field Marshal Fevzi Çakmak was a German-trained battle-tried commander, who had started by opposing Mustafa Kemal, but having decided to side with him, proved a totally loyal Chief of the General Staff during the War of Independence and then to the end of Kemal's life. The fact that he was a pious Muslim did not count against him. Fevzi Pasha was not an enthusiast; he professed the patriotic faith of regimental chaplains. When Mustafa Kemal died, opponents of İsmet's succession wanted to put him up as the candidate allegedly favoured by the first President. He declined, preferring to stay in command of the armed forces. But in the end Fevzi clashed with İsmet, objecting to being retired at the age of 68. He wanted to go on for ever.

On 15 February 1924, Mustafa Kemal and İsmet went to İzmir to watch army manoeuvres and meet military commanders. It was at this meeting that the decision was taken

Turkey and the Near East 1923

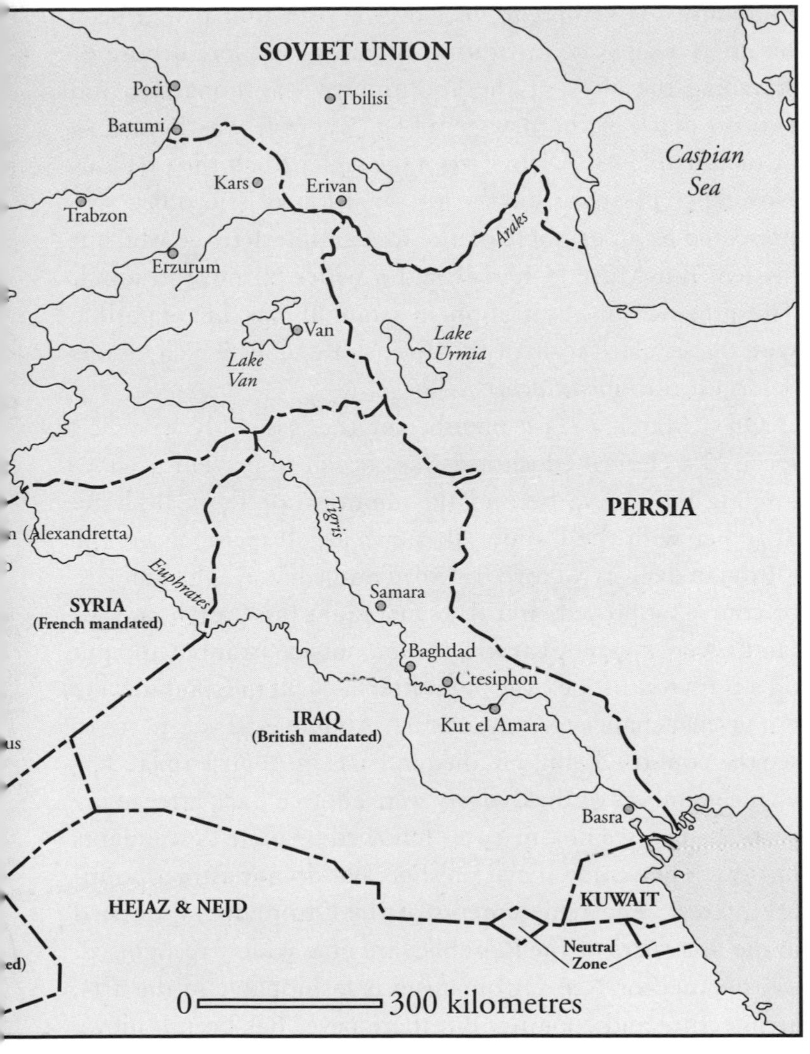
SOVIET UNION
Poti
Tbilisi
Batumi
Kars
Erivan
Trabzon
Caspian Sea
Araks
Erzurum
Van
Lake Van
Lake Urmia
PERSIA
(Alexandretta)
Tigris
Euphrates
SYRIA
(French mandated)
Samara
Baghdad
Ctesiphon
Kut el Amara
IRAQ
(British mandated)
Basra
HEJAZ & NEJD
KUWAIT
Neutral Zone
0 300 kilometres

to abolish the Caliphate, just over a year after it had been set up as a separate institution. It had served its purpose of softening the blow of the abolition of the monarchy, and had no place in the new republic, where it was bound to attract dissidents. A letter from the Agha Khan the previous November pleading for the preservation of the office was presented as an example of the foreign interference which it invited. But Mustafa Kemal had a wider purpose in mind. The presence of the Caliph in Istanbul was incompatible with the secularisation of the Turkish Republic which he was determined to introduce.

On 3 March 1924 a member of the Assembly who had received a clerical education was chosen to present a wide-ranging bill, going beyond the abolition of the Caliphate. Together with the Caliph Abdülmecid, all members of the Ottoman dynasty were to be exiled immediately. The bill was, of course, approved, and the same night the Caliph and his family were taken by car to a station outside Istanbul and put on a train to Europe. Any supporters he had in Istanbul were not given a chance to demonstrate. Abdülmecid was never to see the country again. He died in Paris in August 1944. Surviving members of the dynasty were allowed back after many years, princesses first in 1952, followed by male descendants in 1974. They enjoy social prestige, but do not attract political interest. The achievements of the Ottoman era, decried in the first years of the Republic, are now widely recognised. 'Ottomania' or Neo-Ottomanism is fashionable in the arts, architecture and cooking. But there never has been a movement favouring the restoration of the monarchy in Turkey.

The abolition of the Caliphate was accompanied by the removal of all religious influence on public policy and by the imposition of state control over religious practices. Religious schools (*medrese*) were banned. Religious education in lay schools was restricted and discouraged until it disappeared altogether. The Ministry of Islamic Canonical Affairs and Pious Foundations, which had replaced the office of the Sheikh-al Islam, was abolished and replaced by a Department of Religious Affairs attached to the Office of the Prime Minister. This department employed and supervised mosque personnel, and laid the law on practice and worship. The religious institution had always been under the control of the Ottoman state, but it used to enjoy some autonomy and could at times influence public policy. Now it was totally nationalised.

The nationalist commanders who were excluded from power found a popular cause in public disquiet at the unfolding cultural revolution. Forced to choose between politics and a military career, some of Mustafa Kemal's original companions resigned their commissions and formed an opposition party. They named it the Progressive Republican Party to emphasise that they were not counter-revolutionaries, reactionaries or monarchists. But the promise in the party programme that they would respect religious feelings and beliefs made plain their opposition to the radical transformation of society. In response, Mustafa Kemal adopted a somewhat softer approach. İsmet, known as a hard-line supporter of Mustafa Kemal's radical project, was replaced by the more conciliatory Fethi.

The let-up was short-lived. In February 1925, a Kurdish sheikh raised the standard of rebellion in the east. As the revolt spread, Fethi was seen as hesitant and ineffective. He was replaced by İsmet who this time stayed in power for over a decade. The suppression of the Kurdish rebellion was followed by the banning of the opposition Progressive Republican Party, and by an acceleration of Mustafa Kemal's reform programme. All Dervish orders were banned and their shrines closed. Over the next few years, modernisation became synonymous with westernisation. European laws were introduced wholesale: the Swiss civil code, which put an end to polygamy, German commercial law, the Italian penal code. In November 1925, the fez, which had been for over a century the distinctive headgear of Muslim gentlemen, was banned, and Muslims were ordered to wear European-style hats or peaked caps, both of which are inconvenient when Muslims press their heads against the ground during prayers. A month later the European calendar and European time-keeping replaced the Muslim calendar.

Wilder opponents now took to plotting. In June 1926 an attempt to assassinate Mustafa Kemal in İzmir was narrowly averted when one of the conspirators gave it away. The discovery led to a wave of repression. There was a loose connection between the conspirators and figures of the old CUP who had not accepted Mustafa Kemal's leadership. One such was Cavid, the wartime Ottoman Finance Minister who had advised the Turkish delegation at Lausanne. Critical as he was of Mustafa Kemal, he was not involved in the attempt on his life. Nevertheless, he was hanged along with the conspirators. It was the high-point of state terror.

With all his opponents silenced and the country pacified, Mustafa Kemal could now give his account of the events which had led to the proclamation of the Republic and the subsequent cultural revolution. He did so in October 1927 in a speech to the convention of his Republican People's Party, by then the only party allowed in the country. The speech took six days to deliver. It started with the words: *On the 19th day of May of the year 1919, I landed in Samsun.* Mustafa Kemal's life story had become the history of modern Turkey.

More radical changes followed. In April 1928, the reference to Islam as the official religion was dropped from the constitution. In November that year the last important link with the Muslim Ottoman past was severed when the Latin alphabet replaced the Arabic one. The new alphabet was better suited to the phonetic structure of the Turkish language, and the change was made all the easier by the fact that the vast majority of the population was illiterate, so that most Turks learnt to read and write for the first time in the new script. Other changes were symbolic: Turkish women were given the vote, and some were elected or rather nominated town councillors and then members of parliament in uncontested elections. More importantly, the government encouraged career women. There had long been women teachers in girls' schools. Now there were women teaching in mixed schools and universities, practising medicine and law. The number of professional women grew gradually, although to this day the proportion of women employed outside the home in Turkey is low by European standards. Unlike the fez and clerical dress, the veiling of women was never banned. But it was discouraged and all but disappeared, the veil giving way to headscarves among older women in the cities and, more generally, in the countryside.

In 1934, after a law had been passed that all Turkish citizens should choose surnames in addition to the given Muslim names by which most of them were known, Mustafa Kemal was given the name of Atatürk, Father of the Turks, by the Assembly. The surname was restricted to him alone, and could not be used by his surviving sister or his adopted daughters. His marriage to Lâtife, which was dissolved in 1924, was childless.

Just as the reforms were being completed in Turkey, the

settlement put in place after the First World War was beginning to break down in Europe. The first threat came from the Italian dictator Benito Mussolini. Then, in 1933, Hitler came to power in Germany. Proclaiming *peace at home and peace in the world* as the principle of his foreign policy, Mustafa Kemal sided with the Western democracies in defence of the *status quo*. This allowed Turkey to win back two concessions it had made at Lausanne. In July 1936, a convention was signed at Montreux, abolishing the international commission of the Turkish Straits, allowing Turkish troops back into what had been the demilitarised zone of the Straits, and making Turkey responsible for applying rules for navigation through them. Then, on the eve of the Second World War, in exchange for a treaty of alliance with France and Britain, Turkish troops entered the district of Alexandretta/İskenderun, which had been administered as part of French-Mandated Syria. Renamed the province of Hatay (after Cathay, the area inhabited by Turkic tribes outside the Great Wall of China), the district became part of Turkey some six months after the death of Atatürk on 10 November 1938, at the age of 57. His work of laying the foundations of modern Turkey was completed. The country's subsequent history has shown that the foundations were solid.

Authoritarian by nature, Atatürk was convinced that he alone was always right. After he had consolidated his power, he developed an interest in fashionable dotty theories, such as phrenology. An autodidact in academic subjects, he convinced himself and taught his obedient citizens that the Turks were the ancestors of all civilised peoples and that all languages derived from Turkish. Like nationalists in many other countries he promoted a new language, banishing words of Arabic and Persian (but not West European) origin, and coining new terms from Turkish roots to replace them. At the height of the purification campaign, his pronouncements became unintelligible, but gradually new 'pure' Turkish settled down, developing after his death as a serviceable language, well adapted to express modern concepts, and much simpler and more direct than old 'high' Ottoman – a language made up of Turkish, Persian and Arabic which simple Turks, Persians and Arabs alike were unable to understand. But the change was so radical that Turks today cannot understand the original text of Atatürk's own speeches and writings before the 1930s. He also flirted with racism at a time when racism was widespread not only in Nazi Germany, but throughout the civilised West. But he did not go overboard.

Mustafa Kemal had fought in defence of the Ottoman Empire until it became indefensible, and he inherited the skills and realism of imperial administrators. As a successful military commander, he knew how to adapt his strategy to serve his objective. This was to fashion a united Turkish nation out of the disparate Muslim groups inhabiting the country, to educate them in modern, scientific knowledge, until they joined the mainstream of the one existing human civilisation which happened to have its centre in the West. Unlike most of his predecessors he did not restrict his choice to Western technology. To be as civilised as Westerners, Turks had to think like them, and practice their arts as well as their sciences. Unlike nationalist leaders in recent times, he did not believe in third ways or national forms of civilisation. Unlike most Young Turk politicians, he felt no bitterness towards foreigners, because he believed himself as capable as they were. He had no time for religion, except as a social force to be reckoned with, and believed that people of different religions could find common ground in rationalism.

Unfortunately, many of Atatürk's companions were less open-minded, and were embittered by the real and imagined slights they had endured at the hands of Westerners. Atatürk had set his people the objective of *reaching and then exceeding the level of contemporary civilisation.*[3] But one verse (never sung today) of the national anthem of the Turkish Republic speaks of civilisation as 'a monster with only one tooth left'. What passes for Kemalism today is often a reactive, fearful isolationism expressed in the saying 'The Turk's only friend is another Turk'. Atatürk was not a Kemalist in the sense often used today.

As he prepared to leave Istanbul for Lausanne, the British High Commissioner Sir Horace Rumbold wrote that the spirit which animated the Kemalist Turk 'may be summed up in the expression Asia versus Europe'.[4] He was wrong. Atatürk's vision looked forward to globalisation and a knowledge-based universal civilisation – to the world in which we live today.

Notes

1 Illusions of Power

1. On 9 June 1908 Edward VII and Tsar Nicholas II met in Reval (now Tallinn, capital of Estonia) and agreed that a governor, approved by the European great powers and assisted by a large staff of European advisers, should be appointed for Ottoman Macedonia (Stanford & Ezel Kural Shaw, *History of the Ottoman Empire and Modern Turkey* [CUP: 1977] Vol 2, p 211.)
2. Guenter Lewy, *The Armenian Massacres in Ottoman Turkey: A Disputed Genocide* (Utah UP: 2005) pp 37–9.
3. Population figures and demographic data from Cem Behar (ed.), *The Population of the Ottoman Empire and Turkey* (State Institute of Statistics, Ankara: 1996).
4. Lewy, *The Armenian Massacres*, p 235.
5. The expert was V A Gordelevski, a Russian Turcologist, in a rare Tsarist wartime publication.
6. Justin McCarthy, *The Ottoman Peoples and the End of Empire* (Arnold, London: 2001) pp 171–92.
7. German officers seconded to the Ottoman army were promoted one rank. Hence Generals Liman von Sanders,

Erich von Falkenhayn and Colmar von der Goltz were styled Field Marshal during their service in Turkey.

8. Justin McCarthy, *Muslims and Minorities: The Population of Ottoman Anatolia and the End of the Empire* (New York UP: 1983) pp 50, 52.
9. Justin McCarthy *et al.*, *The Armenian Rebellion at Van* (University of Utah Press: 2006) pp 162–4, 180–5.
10. See Justin McCarthy, *Death and Exile: The Ethnic Cleansing of Ottoman Muslims, 1821–1922* (Darwin Press, Princeton: 1995). For the Circassians and other Muslim refugees from the Caucasus, see pp 32–6, 47–9.
11. Gwynne Dyer, 'The Turkish Armistice of 1918' I, *Middle Eastern Studies* (May 1972) Vol 8, No 2, pp 144–6.
12. www.americanrhetoric.com/speeches/wilsonfourteenpoints.htm
13. Dyer, 'The Turkish Armistice of 1918', p 342, n 2.
14. Dyer, 'The Turkish Armistice of 1918', p 147.
15. Dyer, 'The Turkish Armistice of 1918', p 150.
16. Martin Gilbert, *Sir Horace Rumbold: Portrait of a Diplomat 1869–1941* (Heinemann, London: 1973) p 249.
17. Dyer, 'The Turkish Armistice of 1918', p 159.
18. Mahmud Kemal İnal, *Osmanlı Devrinde Son Sadrıazamlar*, 2nd ed. (Istanbul MEB: 1965) p 2004.
19. Dyer, 'The Turkish Armistice of 1918', pp 153–4.
20. Dyer, 'The Turkish Armistice of 1918', pp 154–6.
21. A J Barker, *The Neglected War: Mesopotamia 1914–1918* (Faber, London: 1967) pp 266, 296. Of the original 9,300 Indian troops, 2,500 perished.
22. Dyer, 'The Turkish Armistice of 1918', p 161.
23. Dyer, 'The Turkish Armistice of 1918', p 166.

24. Mahmud Kemal İnal, *Osmanlı Devrinde Son Sadrıazamlar*, p 2034
25. Dyer, 'The Turkish Armistice of 1918', pp 166–7.
26. Dyer, 'The Turkish Armistice of 1918', p 167.
27. Dyer, 'The Turkish Armistice of 1918', pp 168–9.
28. Edward Erickson, *Ordered to Die: A History of the Ottoman Army in the First World War* (Greenwood, Westport, Conn.: 2001) pp 231–5.
29. Dyer, 'The Turkish Armistice of 1918', pp 336–41.
30. Dyer, 'The Turkish Armistice of 1918', p 337.
31. Cemal Kutay, *Osmanlıdan Cumhuriyete: Yüzyılımızda bir İnsanımız Hüseyin Rauf Orbay (1881–1964)* (Kazancı, Istanbul: 1992) Vol 3, p 174.
32. According to some reports they boarded a torpedo-boat the Germans had captured from the Russians. The date of their flight is given as 8/9 November in some sources. See Andrew Mango, *Atatürk* (John Murray, London: 1999) p 190, n 21.

2 Broken Promises

1. Mango, *Atatürk*, p 191.
2. İhsan Şerif Kaymaz, *Musul Sorun* (Otopsi, Istanbul: 2003) pp 56–7.
3. Mango, *Atatürk*, p 191.
4. Mango, *Atatürk*, pp 191–5.
5. Mango, *Atatürk*, p 196.
6. Maurice Pernot, *La Question turque* (Bernard Grasset, Paris: 1923) pp 90–1.
7. Sina Akşin, *İstanbul Hükümetleri ve Millî Mücadele* (Cem, Istanbul: 1992) Vol 1, p 81.
8. Sina Akşin, *İstanbul Hükümetleri ve Millî Mücadele*, Vol 1, p 198.

9. Sina Akşin, *İstanbul Hükümetleri ve Millî Mücadele*, Vol 1, p 199.
10. Lewy, *The Armenian Massacres*, p 81.
11. Stanford & Ezel Kural Shaw, *History of the Ottoman Empire and Modern Turkey*, p 329.
12. Cemal Kutay, *Osmanlıdan Cumhuriyete*, Vol 3, p 216.
13. David Fromkin, *A Peace to End All Peace* (Deutsch, London: 1989) pp 138–9.
14. David Barchard, 'Out of the Shadows', *Cornucopia* (2008) No 39, p 30.
15. Elie Kedourie, 'Young Turks, Freemasons and Jews' in *Arabic Political Memoirs and other studies* (Frank Cass, London: 1974) p 249.
16. David Gilmour, *Curzon* (John Murray, London: 1994) p 558.
17. Michael Llewellyn Smith, *Ionian Vision* (Allen Lane, London: 1973) p 12.
18. Baskın Oran, *Türk Dış Politikası* (İletişim, Istanbul: 2001) Vol 1, p 99 (illustration).
19. Fromkin, *A Peace to End All Peace*, p 377.
20. Llewellyn Smith, *Ionian Vision*, pp 89–110.

3 Turks Fight for their Rights

1. Kâzım Karabekir, *İstiklâl Harbimiz* (Yapı Kredi, Istanbul: 2008) Vol 1, p 24.
2. Karabekir, *İstiklâl Harbimiz*, Vol 1, p 21.
3. Mango, *Atatürk*, p 216.
4. Murat Bardakçı, *Şahbaba* (Pan Yayıncılık, Istanbul: 1998) p 449.
5. Doğu Ergil, *Milli Mücadelenin Sosyal Tarihi* (Tarhan, Ankara: 1981) p 60.
6. Ergil, *Milli Mücadelenin Sosyal Tarihi*, p 54.

7. Ergil, *Milli Mücadelenin Sosyal Tarihi*, p 65.
8. Llewellyn Smith, *Ionian Vision*, p 71.
9. McCarthy, *Muslims and Minorities*, p 77.
10. Ergil, *Milli Mücadelenin Sosyal Tarihi*, p 94–5.
11. Mahmud Kemal İnal, *Osmanlı Devrinde Son Sadrıazamlar*, p 2040.
12. Sina Akşin, *İstanbul Hükümetleri ve Millî Mücadele*, Vol 1, pp 396–402.
13. Fromkin, *A Peace to End All Peace*, p 385
14. Llewellyn Smith, *Ionian Vision*, pp 123–5.
15. Llewellyn Smith, *Ionian Vision*, p 122.
16. Llewellyn Smith, *Ionian Vision*, p 121.
17. Mahmud Kemal İnal, *Osmanlı Devrinde Son Sadrıazamlar*, pp 1731–2; Baskın Oran, *Türk Dış Politikası*, Vol 1, pp 119–23.
18. Baskın Oran, *Türkiye'nin Dış Politikası*, Vol 1, p 123.
19. Mango, *Atatürk*, p 329.
20. Gilmour, *Curzon*, p 532.
21. Andrew Ryan, *The Last of the Dragomans* (Bles, London: 1951) p 173.
22. http://wilsonforarmenian.am/Report/007Letter.pdf, pp 10–11. It is not surprising that the full text of the Treaty of Sèvres should be available on the internet courtesy of the Hellenic resources network and the Wilson Award thanks to an organisation of Armenian nationalists, 'Wilson for Armenia'.
23. Examples given in Bardakçı, *Şahbaba*, p 162

4 Western Revolution in the East

1. Mango, *Atatürk*, p 345. A single battle – Enver's unsuccessful assault on the Russians in the winter of 1914/15 – cost the Ottoman army 110,000 casualties

(Hikmet Özdemir, *The Ottoman Army 1914–1918* [Utah UP: 2008] p 52.)

2. Mahmud Kemal İnal, *Osmanlı Devrinde Son Sadrıazamlar*, p 2067.
3. Mahmud Kemal İnal, *Osmanlı Devrinde Son Sadrıazamlar*, p 2053.
4. Bardakçı, *Şahbaba*, p 450.
5. Şevket Süreyya Aydemir, *Makedonya'dan Ortaasya'ya Enver Paşa* (Remzi, Istanbul: 1972) Vol 3, pp 549, 574.
6. Taha Akyol, *Ama Hangi Atatürk* (Doğan Kitap, Istanbul: 2008) pp 274–80.
7. Karabekir, *İstiklâl Harbimiz*, Vol 1, p 24.
8. Llewellyn Smith, *Ionian Vision*, p 166.
9. Taha Akyol, *Ama Hangi Atatürk*, pp 289–90. Figures vary in different sources.
10. Mango, *Atatürk*, p 311.
11. Llewellyn Smith, *Ionian Vision*, pp 224, 235.
12. www.tarihogretmeni.net/tarih/diyab-aga-t13218.html
13. Mango, *Atatürk*, p 318.
14. Sami Özerdem, *Atatürk Devrimi Kronolojisi* (Çankaya Belediyesi, Ankara: 1996) p 58.
15. Mango, *Atatürk*, p 321.
16. Llewellyn Smith, *Ionian Vision*, p 232.
17. Llewellyn Smith, *Ionian Vision*, p 203.
18. Gilbert, *Sir Horace Rumbold*, p 243.
19. Gilbert, *Sir Horace Rumbold*, p 243.
20. Gilbert, *Sir Horace Rumbold*, p 249.
21. Llewelleyn Smith, *Ionian Vision*, p 283.
22. Llewelleyn Smith, *Ionian Vision*, p 281.
23. Mango, *Atatürk*, p 340.
24. Mango, *Atatürk*, p 342.

25. İzmir Metropolitan Council, *The City that Rose from the Ashes* (2003) p 15.
26. David Walder, *The Chanak Affair* (Hutchinson, London: 1969) p 177.
27. Cem Behar (ed), *The Population of the Ottoman Empire and Turkey 1500–1927*, pp 2, 64.
28. *Chambers Encyclopaedia* (1904), article on Smyrna.
29. Mark Mazower, *Salonica City of Ghosts* (Harper Collins, London: 2004) p 320.
30. *Atatürk'ün Bütün Eserleri* (Kaynak Yayınları, Istanbul: 2002) Vol 8, p 83.
31. Quoted in Walder, *The Chanak Affair*, p 191.
32. Walder, *The Chanak Affair*, pp 232, 235, 242.
33. Walder, *The Chanak Affair*, p 176.
34. Gilbert, *Sir Horace Rumbold*, p 278.
35. Walder, *The Chanak Affair*, p 289.
36. Alexis Alexandris, *The Greek Minority in Istanbul* (Centre for Asia Minor Studies: Athens 1983) p 104.
37. There were some 1.8 million Greeks in Anatolia (McCarthy, *The Ottoman Peoples and the End of Empire*, p 91). Greek sources put the number of Greeks in Istanbul in 1923 at 250,000 (Alexandris, *The Greek Minority in Istanbul*, p 104), and a similar number of refugees from eastern Thrace resident in Greece in 1928 (McCarthy, *The Ottoman Peoples and the End of Empire*, p 131).
38. Alexandris, *The Greek Minority in Istanbul*, p 141.

5 At One with Civilisation

1. Bardakçı, *Şahbaba*, p 231.
2. Mahmud Kemal İnal, *Osmanlı Devrinde Son Sadrıazamlar*, pp 2097–8.

3. Mango, *Atatürk*, p 364.
4. Mango, *Atatürk*, p 364.
5. Falih Rıfkı Atay, *Çankaya* (Bateş, Istanbul: 1984) p 342.
6. Bardakçı, *Şahbaba*, p 225.
7. Bardakçı, *Şahbaba*, p 244.
8. This account of Vahdettin's departure and the events leading to it is based on Bardakçı, *Şahbaba*, pp 239–54.
9. Mahmud Kemal İnal, *Osmanlı Devrinde Son Sadrıazamlar*, p 2103.
10. Bardakçı, *Şahbaba*, p 241.
11. Philip Mansel, *Sultans in Splendour: The Last Years of the Ottoman World: The Last Days of the Ottoman World* (Andre Deutsch, London: 1988) p 125a.
12. Taha Akyol, *Ama Hangi Atatürk*, p 345.
13. Mustafa Kemal, *Eskişehir-İzmit Konuşmaları (1923)* (Kaynak Yayınları, Istanbul: 1993) p 96.
14. Mustafa Kemal, *Eskişehir-İzmit Konuşmaları*, pp 136, 148.
15. Mustafa Kemal, *Eskişehir-İzmit Konuşmaları*, p 144.
16. *Atatürk'ün Söylev ve Demeçleri* (Atatürk Araştırma Merkezi, Ankara: 1989) Vol 2, p 131.
17. *Atatürk'ün Söylev ve Demeçleri*, Vol 2, p 98.
18. İhan Turan (ed), *İsmet İnönü: Lozan Barış Konferansı* (Atatürk Araştırma Merkezi, Ankara: 2003) p 301.
19. Gilbert, *Sir Horace Rumbold*, p 281.
20. Kemal Atatürk, *Nutuk* (Atatürk Araştırma Merkezi, Ankara: 1989) p 513.
21. Turan (ed), *İsmet İnönü: Lozan Barış Konferansı*, p 305.
22. Gilbert, *Sir Horace Rumbold*, pp 282–3.
23. Turan (ed), *İsmet İnönü: Lozan Barış Konferansı*, p 303.
24. Kemal Atatürk, *Nutuk*, p 524.
25. Kemal Atatürk, *Nutuk*, p 466.

26. www.hri.org/docs/lausanne/part1.html
27. Mustafa Kemal, *Eskişehir-İzmit Konuşmaları* (1923) pp 94–6.

6 Creating a New State and Nation

1. Mango, *Atatürk*, p 394.
2. Kemal Atatürk, *Nutuk*, p 11.
3. Message to the nation on the 10th anniversary of the republic (*Atatürk'ün Söylev ve Demeçleri*, Vol 3, p 318).
4. Gilbert, *Sir Horace Rumbold*, p 276.

Chronology

YEAR	AGE	THE LIFE AND THE LAND
1876–8		Abdülhamid II accedes to Ottoman throne. First constitution proclaimed. Ottomans defeated in war with Russia. Peace treaty signed at Congress of Berlin. Constitution suspended.
1881		Mustafa Kemal born in Salonica.
1895	14	Ottoman liberals meet in Paris and form Society (later Committee) of Union and Progress to lead struggle for return to constitutional rule.
1908	27	24 Jul: Ottoman troops mutiny in Macedonia and force Abdülhamid II to reintroduce the constitution.
1909	28	13 Apr: Soldiers mutiny in Istanbul ('Incident of 31 March', Julian calendar) and chase out CUP. Troops assembled by the latter enter Istanbul and depose Abdülhamid II, who is succeeded by Mehmed V Reşad.
1911	30	Italy invades Libya. Enver and Mustafa Kemal organise resistance to the invaders.

YEAR	HISTORY	CULTURE
1876–8	Queen Victoria proclaimed Empress of India. Satsuma rebellion suppressed in Japan.	Thomas Hardy, *The Return of the Native*. Algernon Charles Swinburne, *Poems and Ballads*. Ruskin-Whistler libel case.
1881	First Boer War.	Henry James, *Portrait of a Lady*.
1895	Sino-Japanese War ends. Jameson Raid into Transvaal. Cuba rebels against Spanish rule.	H G Wells, *The Time Machine*. W B Yeats, *Poems*. Tchaikovsky, ballet *Swan Lake*.
1908	*The Daily Telegraph* publishes remarks about German hostility towards England made by Kaiser Wilhelm II.	E M Forster, *A Room with a View*.
1909	King Edward VII dies; succeeded by George V. Liberals win General Election.	Karl May, *Winnetou*. Puccini, *La Fanciulla del West*.
1911	Arrival of German gunboat *Panther* in Agadir triggers international crisis. Peter Stolypyn, Russian Premier, assassinated.	Max Beerbohm, *Zuleika Dobson*. D H Lawrence, *The White Peacock*.

YEAR	AGE	THE LIFE AND THE LAND
1912–13	31–2	The Balkan states declare war. The Ottoman army is defeated and retreats to the outskirts of Istanbul. The CUP seizes power in a coup. Enver becomes War Minister.
1914	33	Enver authorises German warships flying the Turkish flag to attack the Russians. Nov: The Allies declare war on the Ottomans.
1915	34	18 Mar: Allied fleet fails to force a passage through the Dardanelles. 25 Apr: Anzacs and British troops land in Gallipoli. Mustafa Kemal distinguishes himself in battles on the peninsula. Armenian deportations begin as Russian army advances into eastern Turkey.
1916	35	9 Jan: Allies evacuate Gallipoli. Promoted Brigadier, Mustafa Kemal is posted first to eastern front to fight the Russians, then to Syria against the British. He resigns his command after quarrelling with the Germans.

YEAR	HISTORY	CULTURE
1912–13	*Titanic* sinks. Woodrow Wilson is elected US President.	Thomas Mann, *Death in Venice.* Marcel Proust, *Du côté de chez Swann.* Grand Central Station in New York is completed.
1914	Archduke Franz Ferdinand of Austria-Hungary and his wife are assassinated in Sarajevo. Outbreak of First World War: Battles of Mons, the Marne and First Ypres, Tannenberg and Masurian Lakes.	James Joyce, *Dubliners.* Theodore Dreiser, *The Titan.* Gustav Holst, *The Planets.* Matisse, *The Red Studio.* Braque, *Music.* Film: Charlie Chaplin in *Making a Living.*
1915	First World War: Battles of Neuve Chapelle and Loos. The 'Shells Scandal'. Germans sink the British liner *Lusitania,* killing 1,198.	Joseph Conrad, *Victory.* John Buchan, *The Thirty-Nine Steps.* Ezra Pound, *Cathay.* Film: *The Birth of a Nation.*
1916	First World War. Battle of Verdun. The Battle of the Somme. The Battle of Jutland. US President Woodrow Wilson is re-elected. Wilson issues Peace Note to belligerents in European war. Lloyd George becomes British Prime Minister.	James Joyce, *Portrait of an Artist as a Young Man.* Film: *Intolerance.*

YEAR	AGE	THE LIFE AND THE LAND
1918	37	Mustafa Kemal accompanies heir apparent Vahdettin on a visit to the Western Front. 3 Jul: Sultan Mehmed V dies and is succeeded by Vahdettin who assumes name of Mehmed VI. Aug: Mustafa Kemal returns to command in Syria. Sep: Mustafa Kemal forced to move his headquarters to Aleppo as the British break through the Ottoman front in Palestine. 30 Oct: The Ottoman government sues for peace and signs armistice in Mudros Bay. CUP leaders escape from Istanbul, Mustafa Kemal returns to the capital and seeks appointment as War Minister.
1919	38	19 May: Mustafa Kemal secures appointment as inspector-general of Ottoman troops in eastern Turkey and lands in Samsun four days after Greek troops land in İzmir/Smyrna. 17 Jun: Grand Vizier Damad Ferid sets out his position on peace terms in a memorandum to the Allies in Paris. Jul–Sep: Turkish nationalists hold congresses in Erzurum, then in Sivas. Mustafa Kemal, elected Chairman of Permanent Executive, moves to Ankara.

YEAR	HISTORY	CULTURE
1918	First World War. Peace Treaty of Brest-Litovsk between Russia and the Central Powers. German Spring offensives on Western Front fail. Allied offensives on Western Front have German army in full retreat. Armistice signed between Allies and Germany; German Fleet surrenders. Kaiser Wilhelm II of Germany abdicates.	Alexander Blok, *The Twelve.* Gerald Manley Hopkins, *Poems.* Luigi Pirandello, *Six Characters in Search of an Author.* Bela Bartok, *Bluebeard's Castle.* Puccini, *Il Trittico*. Gustav Cassel, *Theory of Social Economy.* Kokoshka, *Friends* and *Saxonian Landscape.* Edvard Munch, *Bathing Man.*
1919	Communist Revolt in Berlin. Paris Peace Conference adopts principle of founding League of Nations. Benito Mussolini founds fascist movement in Italy. Peace Treaty of Versailles signed. US Senate votes against ratification of Versailles Treaty, leaving the USA outside the League of Nations.	Bauhaus movement founded by Walter Gropius. Thomas Hardy, *Collected Poems.* George Bernard Shaw, *Heartbreak House.* Film: *The Cabinet of Dr Caligari.*

YEAR	AGE	THE LIFE AND THE LAND
1920	39	Elections held. Last Ottoman parliament meets in Istanbul and endorses National Pact demanding Turkey's independence within 1918 armistice lines. 18 Mar: Allies complete occupation of Istanbul. 23 Apr: National Assembly meets in Ankara and elects Mustafa Kemal President. 10 Aug: Sultan's government signs Treaty of Sèvres, as Greek troops occupy western Anatolia. Sep/Dec: Turkish national army defeats the Armenians and secures country's eastern frontier. Nov: Venizelos is defeated in Greek elections. King Constantine returns.
1921	40	Jan: İsmet stops Greek advance at İnönü. Feb: Conference in London fails to agree revision of Treaty of Sèvres. Mar: Ankara government signs treaty of friendship with Russia. Apr: Greeks stopped again at second Battle of İnönü. Jul: Greeks break through Turkish lines and advance to Sakarya river. 5 Aug: Assembly appoints Mustafa Kemal Commander-in-Chief. He forces the Greeks back at the Battle of Sakarya. 20 Oct: France signs preliminary peace treaty with Ankara government and evacuates southern Turkey. Italian occupation troops withdraw.

YEAR	HISTORY	CULTURE
1920	League of Nations comes into existence. The Hague is selected as seat of International Court of Justice. League of Nations headquarters is moved to Geneva. Warren G Harding wins US Presidential election. Bolsheviks win Russian Civil War. Government of Ireland Act is passed. Adolf Hitler announces his 25-point programme in Munich.	F Scott Fitzgerald, *This Side of Paradise.* Franz Kafka, *The Country Doctor.* Katherine Mansfield, *Bliss.* Rambert School of Ballet formed. Lyonel Feininger, *Church.* Juan Gris, *Book and Newspaper.* Vincent D'Indy, *The Legend Of St Christopher.* Maurice Ravel, *La Valse.*
1921	Irish Free State established. Peace treaty signed between Russia and Germany. State of Emergency proclaimed in Germany in the face of economic crisis. Washington Naval Treaty signed.	Aldous Huxley, *Chrome Yellow.* D H Lawrence, *Women in Love.* Prokofiev, *The Love for Three Oranges.*

YEAR	AGE	THE LIFE AND THE LAND
1922	41	30 Aug: Turkish troops destroy the Greek army in western Anatolia. 9 Sep: Turkish army enters İzmir. Sep/Oct: 'Chanak Affair' as Turkish troops press against the neutral zone of the Straits, defended by the British. 11 Oct: Armistice between Turkey and the Allies signed at Mudanya. Greeks evacuate eastern Thrace. 1 Nov: Assembly in Ankara abolishes the Sultanate, keeping the Caliphate. 17 Nov: Mehmed VI Vahdettin escapes from Istanbul on British warship. Assembly deposes him as Caliph and chooses heir apparent Abdülmecid to succeed him. 21 Nov: Peace conference opens in Lausanne.
1923	42	4 Feb: Lausanne Conference is suspended, after Turkey and Greece agree on exchange of populations. 23 Apr: Lausanne Conference resumes. 23 Jul: Peace is signed at Lausanne. 2 Oct: Allies evacuate Istanbul. Ankara becomes Turkey's capital. 29 Oct: Turkish Republic is proclaimed by the National Assembly. Mustafa Kemal is elected first President.
1924	43	3 Mar: Caliphate is abolished, and all members of the Ottoman dynasty are banished. Secularisation of Turkish state proceeds rapidly.

YEAR	HISTORY	CULTURE
1922	Britain recognises Kingdom of Egypt under Fuad I. Election in Irish Free State gives majority to Pro-Treaty candidates. IRA takes large areas under its control. League of Nations Council approves British Mandate in Palestine.	T S Eliot, *The Waste Land.* James Joyce, *Ulysses.* F Scott Fitzgerald, *The Beautiful and Damned.* British Broadcasting Company (later Corporation) (BBC) founded: first radio broadcasts.
1923	French and Belgian troops occupy the Ruhr when Germany fails to make reparation payments. The USSR formally comes into existence. Wilhelm Marx succeeds Stresemann as German Chancellor. State of Emergency declared in Germany. British Mandate in Palestine begins. Adolf Hitler's *coup d'état* (The Beer Hall Putsch) fails.	P G Wodehouse, *The Inimitable Jeeves.* George Gershwin, *Rhapsody in Blue.* Bela Bartok, *Dance Suite.* BBC listings magazine *Radio Times* first published.
1924	Death of Lenin. Dawes Plan published. Greece is proclaimed a republic.	Noel Coward, *The Vortex.* E M Forster, *A Passage to India.* Thomas Mann, *The Magic Mountain.* George Bernard Shaw, *St Joan.*

YEAR	AGE	THE LIFE AND THE LAND
1925	44	Jun: Opposition to Mustafa Kemal is suppressed following Kurdish rebellion in the east. İsmet becomes Prime Minister and holds office until Oct 1937. Reforms proceed with ban on fez and adoption of Western laws.
1926	45	5 Jun: Treaty signed with Britain establishing Turkey's south-eastern frontier. Iraq keeps Mosul. 15 Jun: Discovery of attempt to assassinate Mustafa Kemal in İzmir leads to new wave of repression. Prominent CUP members executed.
1927	46	15–20 Oct: Mustafa Kemal gives his account of the birth of the Turkish Republic and of the reforms at a convention of his Republican People's Party, which retains power until 1950.
1928	47	Mention of Islam as official religion removed from the constitution.
1929	48	1 Nov: Turkey adopts the Latin Alphabet.
1930	49	Greek leader Venizelos visits Ankara and signs friendship treaty with Turkey.
1933	52	Republic celebrates 10th anniversary. Mustafa Kemal proclaims objective of 'reaching and then surpassing the level of contemporary civilisation'.
1934	53	Surnames made compulsory. Mustafa Kemal chooses surname of Atatürk (Father of the Turks).

YEAR	HISTORY	CULTURE
1925	Pound Sterling returns to the Gold Standard. Paul von Hindenburg, former military leader, is elected President of Germany. Locarno Treaty signed in London.	Franz Kafka, *The Trial.* Virginia Woolf, *Mrs Dalloway.* Film: *Battleship Potemkin.*
1926	General Strike in Great Britain. France proclaims the Lebanon as a republic. Germany is admitted into the League of Nations.	A A Milne, *Winnie the Pooh.* Ernest Hemingway, *The Sun Also Rises.* Film: *The General.*
1927	Inter-Allied military control of Germany ends. Britain recognises rule of Ibn Saud in the Hejaz.	Marcel Proust, *Le Temps retrouvé.* Adolf Hitler, *Mein Kampf.* Film: *The Jazz Singer.*
1928	Transjordan becomes self-governing under the British Mandate.	D H Lawrence, *Lady Chatterley's Lover.*
1929	The Wall Street Crash	Erich Maria Remarque, *All Quiet on the Western Front.*
1930	The United Kingdom, France, Italy, Japan and the US sign the London Naval Treaty regulating naval expansion.	Noel Coward, *Private Lives.*
1933	Adolf Hitler is appointed Chancellor of Germany. Germany withdraws from League of Nations and Disarmament Conference.	George Orwell, *Down and Out in Paris and London.* Films: *Duck Soup. King Kong. Queen Christina.*
1934	Germany, 'Night of the Long Knives'. Hitler becomes *Führer.*	Robert Graves, *I, Claudius.* Film: *David Copperfield.*

YEAR	AGE	THE LIFE AND THE LAND
1936	55	20 Jul: Montreux Convention is signed, allowing Turkish army back into the zone of the Straits, abolishing the international commission and making Turkey responsible for regulating free navigation.
1937	56	District of Alexandretta becomes self-governing under agreement with France. (Turkish troops enter it on 5 Jul 1938, and on 29 Jun 1939 local parliament votes to join Turkey.)
1938	57	10 Nov: Atatürk dies in Istanbul. İsmet İnönü succeeds him as second President of the Turkish Republic.

YEAR	HISTORY	CULTURE
1936	German troops occupy Rhineland. Abdication Crisis in the UK. Outbreak of Spanish Civil War.	J M Keynes, *General Theory of Employment, Interest and Money.* BBC begins world's first television transmission service.
1937	UK Royal Commission on Palestine recommends partition into British and Arab areas and Jewish state. Italy joins German-Japanese Anti-Comintern Pact.	Jean-Paul Sartre, *La Nausée.* John Steinbeck, *Of Mice and Men.* Films: *Snow White and the Seven Dwarfs. A Star is Born. La Grande Illusion.*
1938	German troops enter Austria which is declared part of the German Reich.	Graham Greene, *Brighton Rock.* Film: *Alexander Nevsky.*

Further Reading

There are two recent short histories of modern Turkey: Erik Zurcher's *Turkey A Modern History* (revised edition, paperback, I.B.Tauris, London: 2004) and Sina Akşin's *Turkey From Empire To Revolutionary Republic* (Hurst, London: 2007). My own *Atatürk* (John Murray, London: 1999) and its sequel *The Turks Today* (John Murray, London: 2004) relate the birth and development of the Turkish Republic. For more detailed treatment consult Reşat Kasaba (ed), *The Cambridge History of Turkey, v.4, Turkey in the Modern World* (CUP: 2008) and Caroline Finkel, *Osman's Dream: The Story of the Ottoman Empire 1300–1923* (John Murray, London: 2005). Alan Palmer's *The Decline and Fall of the Ottoman Empire* (John Murray, London: 1992) provides a readable non-academic treatment of the subject.

The best and most recent concise history of the First World War is Norman Stone's *World War I: A Short History* (Allen Lane, London 2007). There are more specialized books on Turkey's participation in the War. Ulrich Trumpener's *Germany and the Ottoman Empire 1914–1918* (Princeton University Press: 1968) remains a classic. Consult also Edward Erickson, *Ordered to Die: A History of the Ottoman Army in the First World War* (Greenwood Press, Westport, Conn.: 2001) and Hikmet Özdemir, *The Ottoman Army 1914–1918: Disease and Death on the Battlefield* (University of Utah: 2008). There are several studies of the Gallipoli campaign, the best known being Alan Moorehead's *Gallipoli* (latest reprint of paperback, Aurum Press, London: 2007). The British campaign in Mesopotamia is described in A J Barker's *The Neglected War* (Faber & Faber, London: 1967). For the 1922 Chanak Crisis, consult David Walder, *The Chanak Affair* (Hutchinson, London: 1969). The highly controversial subject of the Armenian deportations is ably covered in Guenter Lewy's *The Armenian Massacres in Ottoman Turkey: A Disputed Genocide* (University of Utah, Salt Lake City: 2005). The Allies' Near Eastern diplomacy is the subject of David Fromkin's *A Peace to End All Peace* (André Deutsch, London: 1989). Michael Llewellyn Smith's *Ionian Vision: Greece and Asia Minor 1919–1922* (Allen Lane, London: 1973) is impartial and readable.

There are two English-language academic studies of İsmet İnönü: Faruk Loğoğlu, *İsmet İnönü and the Making of Modern Turkey* (İnönü Vakfı, Ankara: 1997) and Metin Heper, *İsmet İnönü, Turkish Diplomat and Statesman* (Brill, Leiden: 1998). Enver Pasha awaits his English-language biographer. For biographies of the major British participants in the Near Eastern peace settlement, consult David Gilmour's *Curzon* (John Murray, London: 1994) and Martin Gilbert's *Sir Horace Rumbold: Portrait of a Diplomat 1869–1941* (Heinemann, London: 1973). Lively eye-witness accounts of Istanbul at the end of the First World War will be found in Andrew Ryan's *The Last of the Dragomans* (Geoffrey Bles, London: 1951) and John G Bennett, *Witness* (Omen, Tucson, Arizona: 1974).

Picture Sources

The author and publishers wish to express their thanks to the following sources of illustrative material and/or permission to reproduce it. They will make proper acknowledgements in future editions in the event that any omissions have occurred.

Corbis Images: p xii. akg Images: pp 104, 178.

Endpapers

The Signing of Peace in the Hall of Mirrors, Versailles, 28th June 1919 by Sir William Orpen (Imperial War Museum: Bridgeman Art Library)
Front row: Dr Johannes Bell (Germany) signing with Herr Hermann Müller leaning over him
Middle row (seated, left to right): General Tasker H Bliss, Col E M House, Mr Henry White, Mr Robert Lansing, President Woodrow Wilson (United States); M Georges Clemenceau (France); Mr David Lloyd George, Mr Andrew Bonar Law, Mr Arthur J Balfour, Viscount Milner, Mr G N Barnes (Great Britain); Prince Saionji (Japan)
Back row (left to right): M Eleftherios Venizelos (Greece);

Dr Afonso Costa (Portugal); Lord Riddell (British Press); Sir George E Foster (Canada); M Nikola Pašić (Serbia); M Stephen Pichon (France); Col Sir Maurice Hankey, Mr Edwin S Montagu (Great Britain); the Maharajah of Bikaner (India); Signor Vittorio Emanuele Orlando (Italy); M Paul Hymans (Belgium); General Louis Botha (South Africa); Mr W M Hughes (Australia)

Jacket images

(Front): Corbis Images: akg Images.
(Back): *Peace Conference at the Quai d'Orsay* by Sir William Orpen (Imperial War Museum: akg Images).
Left to right (seated): Signor Orlando (Italy); Mr Robert Lansing, President Woodrow Wilson (United States); M Georges Clemenceau (France); Mr David Lloyd George, Mr Andrew Bonar Law, Mr Arthur J Balfour (Great Britain); Left to right (standing): M Paul Hymans (Belgium); Mr Eleftherios Venizelos (Greece); The Emir Feisal (The Hashemite Kingdom); Mr W F Massey (New Zealand); General Jan Smuts (South Africa); Col E M House (United States); General Louis Botha (South Africa); Prince Saionji (Japan); Mr W M Hughes (Australia); Sir Robert Borden (Canada); Mr G N Barnes (Great Britain); M Ignacy Paderewski (Poland)

Index

UK PUBLICATION: November 2008 to December 2010
CLASSIFICATION: Biography/History/
International Relations
FORMAT: 198 × 128mm
EXTENT: 208pp
ILLUSTRATIONS: 6 photographs plus 4 maps
TERRITORY: world

Chronology of life in context, full index, bibliography innovative layout with sidebars

Woodrow Wilson: United States of America by Brian Morton
Friedrich Ebert: Germany by Harry Harmer
Georges Clemenceau: France by David Watson
David Lloyd George: Great Britain by Alan Sharp
Prince Saionji: Japan by Jonathan Clements
Wellington Koo: China by Jonathan Clements
Eleftherios Venizelos: Greece by Andrew Dalby
From the Sultan to Atatürk: Turkey by Andrew Mango
The Hashemites: The Dream of Arabia by Robert McNamara
Chaim Weizmann: The Dream of Zion by Tom Fraser
Piip, Meierovics & Voldemaras: Estonia, Latvia & Lithuania by Charlotte Alston
Ignacy Paderewski: Poland by Anita Prazmowska
Beneš, Masaryk: Czechoslovakia by Peter Neville
Károlyi & Bethlen: Hungary by Bryan Cartledge
Karl Renner: Austria by Jamie Bulloch
Vittorio Orlando: Italy by Spencer Di Scala
Pašić & Trumbić: The Kingdom of Serbs, Croats and Slovenes by Dejan Djokic
Aleksandŭr Stamboliĭski: Bulgaria by R J Crampton
Ion Bratianu: Romania by Keith Hitchin
Paul Hymans: Belgium by Sally Marks
General Smuts: South Africa by Antony Lentin
William Hughes: Australia by Carl Bridge
William Massey: New Zealand by James Watson
Sir Robert Borden: Canada by Martin Thornton
Maharajah of Bikaner: India by Hugh Purcell
Afonso Costa: Portugal by Filipe Ribeiro de Meneses
Epitácio Pessoa: Brazil by Michael Streeter
South America by Michael Streeter
Central America by Michael Streeter
South East Asia by Andrew Dalby
The League of Nations by Ruth Henig
Consequences of Peace: The Versailles Settlement – Aftermath and Legacy by Alan Sharp